Supplementary Volume no. 8

TRADE AND FAMINE
IN CLASSICAL ANTIQUITY

PETER GARNSEY
AND
C. R. WHITTAKER

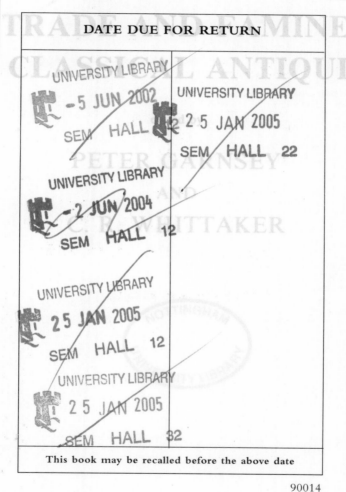

THE CAMBRIDGE PHILOLOGICAL SOCIETY
1983

ISBN 0 906014 04 2

100261198

Printed in Great Britain by the University Press, Cambridge

CONTENTS

PREFACE

The theme of the Ancient History (Greece and Rome) Section of the 8th International Economic History Congress, held in Budapest from August 16-20, 1982, was Trade in Staples (Commerce en articles de base). A 'famine component' was built into the session in order to bring it into contact with one of the main themes of the Congress. P. Garnsey took part in the preparations for the Open Forum on Famine which culminated in a colloquium on Famine in History at Vevey, Switzerland, in June, 1982. The papers for the section (B 12) were submitted in December 1982 and published in advance of the Congress by the Akadémiai Kiadó, as a separate booklet together with some papers from the Ancient Near East Section (B 11). Most of the papers appear in the present volume in a revised version; one, by P. Middleton, fills a gap left unexpectedly vacant in the original publication.

We owe warm thanks to our chairmen at the Congress, Professors Heinz Kreissig and Keith Hopkins, and to our local host Professor István Hahn.

P. G.
C. R. W

March 1983

1. INTRODUCTION

This volume gives a new twist to the current debate over trade in the ancient world. It offers as a basic premise that climate and geography in combination with socio-political conditions ensured a substantial medium-range trade in staples in classical antiquity.

For present purposes staples stands for staple foodstuffs, principally grain, but also wine and olive oil. A second group of staples, consisting of metals, wood for fuel and construction, other building materials, salt, and so on, is not considered here. This is regrettable, for the 'commercial history' of the two tiers of staples comes together at a number of points. For that matter, trade in luxuries too is not necessarily separable from trade in essentials, as for example when Egyptian or Sicilian grain was exchanged for precious metals. But it seemed advantageous to organise a conference session, and a publication, around the twin focal points of trade and famine – where trade stands for trade in essential foodstuffs, and famine for critical shortage of these items.

Surplus foodstuffs were carried short distances by producers supplying a local market. But they were also transported longer distances and in bulk, in order to make up deficiencies in supply. There were, on the one hand, permanent deficiencies. Not all areas within the Mediterranean basin, let alone within the Graeco-Roman world, can produce olive oil, just as not all are rich in mineral resources or capable of producing from local resources sufficient textiles for the home market. On the other hand, there were temporary deficiencies which occurred regularly, though unpredictably. A common cause was harvest failure or shortfall in one year or in a succession of years. (Equally unpredictably, a deficiency in one year could be turned into a considerable surplus in the next.) The high level of variability in climate, the major cause of the high level of variability in crop yield, affected all areas, including Sicily, North Africa and the Black Sea region. These, together with Egypt, constituted the main surplus-producing areas in the case of grain. Egypt too suffered from recurring fluctuations in harvest levels, though these were much less severe than elsewhere, and were related to the height of the Nile flood rather than *local* climatic conditions. But even where there was no absolute shortage of grain, local food crises could occur as a result of a variety of human causes, ranging from warfare to hoarding and speculation, which led in turn to a breakdown of distribution systems.

The notion that a combination of natural and man-made shortages gave rise to a bulk movement of staples beyond the locality is not irreconcileable with an influential doctrine which at first sight might seem to point in another direction: autarky, the self-sufficiency of groups and communities, the capacity of consumers

2

to feed themselves as producers, or to be fed by dependents. The ideology of autarky might be complementary rather than conflicting. If self-sufficiency was a goal that was often approached but not generally achieved, then the shortfall or deficiency, which could only be made up from the surplus of others, became regular.

How far did famine or food shortage generate trade? Is it the case that most staples transported in non-local, inter-town trade moved in consequence of harvest fluctuations? This hypothesis is proposed but not comprehensively tested in this volume. A full treatment must await further studies, which moreover will have to assemble modern as well as ancient data. The only statistically significant data relevant to climatic variability and harvest fluctuation are modern.

Two papers consider the relation between trade and famine in specific historical contexts (while others touch on the issue). Rathbone argues that a marked increase in wheat exports from Egypt from the early third century B.C. would have eased the problem of supply for the Greek cities of the Hellenistic East – always supposing that in this period of constant warfare the grain shipments could get through; while Whittaker concludes that population growth in the trans-frontier regions in the period of late antiquity, partly as a consequence of trade contacts with the Roman empire, led to food shortages, increased pressure on the frontiers, and eventually to the breakdown of the frontier system in the third and fourth centuries A.D. There are in addition two papers exploring the subject of famine over a somewhat wider range. Jameson provides a general study of famine centred on the Greek world, Garnsey a case study of the institutional response to food shortage in the largest and best-known city of antiquity, Rome. These are introductory papers. But some of the conclusions may well surprise and provoke. There is no evidence of general shortages, no evidence, one might almost say, of famine at the level of a 'natural disaster', in the Greek world. Peasants could on the whole subsist. That is the lesson driven home by Jameson. One might perhaps expect that urban artisans and wage-labourers, and the non-citizen element of the population of cities, were more vulnerable to food crisis, but even so there is no record which compels us to believe that there were actual catastrophes in an urban setting. Food crises in the city of Rome were, similarly, relatively rare and never very serious, not at any rate after the early period. This is consistent with the view that the food supply of Rome, once it became an imperial city dominating the Mediterranean, was essentially a logistical matter, a problem of distributing stocks of grain which were never lacking. But the 'mildness' of Rome's food crises should not blind us to the conspicuous shortcomings of the system of supply and distribution that operated in the city.

Famine in antiquity is largely uncharted territory. With trade, on the other hand, we are back again in familiar terrain, albeit one which often refuses to reveal its secrets. A basic question is the following: Did staples travel in significant quantities and over long distances? Morel is concerned to undermine some common assumptions about long-distance trade in staples. He argues, with reference to traffic in wine, that the picture has been distorted by popular misconceptions concerning the geographical origins of pottery, and, consequently, that there have been radical miscalculations about the distance travelled by pots between workshop and findspot. Imitations locally produced were ubiquitous, and branches played a significant role in the diffusion of pottery. Between vigorous local trade, and a downgraded category of long-distance trade, he inserts a category of intensive exchanges over shorter distances – 10-100 km, or further by sea. Hopkins, who is operating with broadly similar categories, also emphasizes on the one hand the primacy of local trade, and on the other the vigour of intra-regional trade, which, he conjectures, supplied up to 10% of the needs of average towns. This medium-range trade was essentially carried out by sea or navigable river. This is indisputable, even if (as Hopkins argues) the cost differential between land and water transport was somewhat narrower than has been thought and the contrast between inland and coastal cities less sharp – for only non-economic assets (basically political power) could permit a city, wherever situated, to grow beyond the food-producing capacity of its territory. The major cities, Rome, Alexandria, Antioch, Carthage, were in another class, being obliged at all times to acquire some of their staples from outside the immediate hinterland, and indeed the region. Beyond the feeding of imperial capitals – and imperial armies – and major provincial cities, it is hard to see a long-distance trade in staples developing in any but exceptional cases – such as the extraordinary export of Italian wine to pre-conquest Gaul, which is associated with the flowering of slave production in central Italy from the late-second to the mid-first century B.C.

It is impossible to discuss the long-range transport of staples without broaching the topic of the nature of the operation: what economic and political forces were at work? It is commonly held that when consumer goods *are* found to have travelled long distances, the context is clearly defined and does not include straightforward commercial exchange (we leave aside the vexed question of how this concept might be precisely defined in the ancient context). The explanation is invariably administrative/political: goods move by the direction of the political authorities, most obviously to supply an imperial city or the armies of a controlling power. Hopkins, however, insists on a role for private trade in the provisioning of major urban centres, including Rome. Similarly, Morel, in holding that the Gallic clients of Italian wine merchants in the Republican period (in contrast with the imperial period) were essentially civilian, appears to be siding with A. Tchernia (in *Trade in the ancient economy*, Garnsey, Hopkins, Whittaker (edd.) (1983)) against an extreme statement of the administrative/political thesis. On the other hand, Middleton in this volume, while accepting the importance of the civilian trade in Gaul, argues that it was dependent on military supplies and consumption. That the trade in question was exceptional is not disputed.

Other matters treated in this volume, notably the personnel involved in trade (what was their social status, economic condition and political influence?), and the pattern and geographical context of trade, cannot be completely divorced from the issue just raised of the nature of the operation. Two contributors consider the personnel of trade, one directly, the other indirectly. Bravo's position on trade in archaic Greece, that it was dominated by landowners directly or through dependents, is a plausible, while ultimately unprovable hypothesis. There are simply too many gaps in the evidence. For example, one cannot rule out a category of traders who were not dependent on the wealthy. Certainly the absence of any evidence for bottomry loans for the archaic period, in other words, lack of information about the way independent traders might have financed their ventures, is not a valid argument against their existence. The earliest attested bottomry loan (of 421 B.C.) was surely not the first. In the Roman period, what is in dispute is not the status of traders (who were undeniably 'small-fry'), but that of shipowners and investors in trade. Hopkins argues that large ships, especially those which carried grain to Rome, were so expensive to build that they must be taken to represent a substantial investment which only wealthy individuals (or, one might add, corporations) could afford. The controversial question of the involvement of the Roman upper classes in trade is thus raised once more.

If the personnel of trade remains a matter for debate, there is much that is uncertain also about the pattern of trade. Variability of crop yield, both within and between regions must have hampered the development of regular supply lines in all periods. No more so than in the Greek archaic age. This was a society which knew limited urban growth, in which therefore state mechanisms for directing and controlling trade in staples were virtually absent. Hesiod's words 'If you should turn your foolish mind to *emporia* and wish to escape from debt and painful *limos*' (*Works and Days* 646-7) capture the spirit of the age. The grain trade and the easing of famine were an individual affair, with the *polis* remaining on the sidelines. The limited nature of Solon's law forbidding the export of agricultural produce apart from oil (Plut. *Sol.* 24) needs to be stressed. Its intention was basically to deny the rich the free disposal of their cornstocks. The well-known law from Teos (Meiggs-Lewis 30) was probably similarly motivated, but it belongs to the early fifth century B.C., a hundred years after Solon.

Urban growth and the development of naval empire transform the picture in the classical period. We have however little detailed information on trade. Garlan's paper on the character of trade between the Ukraine and Thasos suggests a world of merchant adventurers and politically restricted ports of trade, not open markets. Aristotle's epigram 'Food comes to the rulers of the seas' (*Ath. Pol.* 2.6) implies that Athenian trade at any rate had gained a new regularity and system dependent on its political power. The consequences for other states in the Aegean which lacked such influence are unclear. Those which had established trading links would have doubtless done their utmost to keep them intact. Thus it is written into a treaty between Clazomenai and an Athens beginning to reassert itself after the calamitous Peloponnesian War, that Clazomenai in the event of food shortage (*sitodeia*) would continue to be able to seek help in certain cities, including Smyrna (Tod II 114, 387 B.C.). The Hellenistic period should have brought relief to cities such as Clazomenai with circumscribed territories, if we follow Rathbone in holding that wheat exports from Egypt increased substantially from about 280 B.C. Rathbone like Jameson finds no reason to suppose that there were disastrous shortages, and he concludes that prices in general must have dropped, thus providing less scope for manipulation by landowners and merchants. Rathbone himself indicates the difficulty of substantiating this theory, given the patchy evidence available on food prices and our ignorance of the behaviour of other sources of supply and markets for Mediterranean grain in this period.

By the turn of the era, Rome controlled most of the surplus of the main grain-producing areas of the Mediterranean, having lately acquired Egypt and the rich grain lands of the Danube delta. The consequences must have been momentous for the populations of the empire, particularly for the inhabitants of the Eastern Mediterranean in the early Principate. The matter is raised but not investigated in this volume. Whittaker does however discuss the changing fortunes of one important group on the outer edge of the Roman world, whose behaviour was destined to have more than peripheral significance in the late Empire: that is, the 'barbarians' of what he calls the 'buffer' zones across the frontiers, who were linked by trade relationships with the populations on the Roman side. The cycle of population growth, food shortage and emigration was not new to antiquity – it was as old as the demographic movements of the 'dark' and early archaic ages of Greece – but in the collapse of the Western Roman Empire it achieved its most startling result.

In the end questions about food and famine come down to the land, the relation of producers to the land, and the uses to which land was put. Modern studies, in particular that of A. Sen (*Poverty and Famines* (1981)), have underlined the fact that famine is characterized not by an absolute shortage of food, but rather an inability of some communities and some groups within them to attract or control such supplies as are available. In antiquity one can pinpoint periods of change in which some sectors of the population suffered reduced access to food supplies as a result of a breakdown of social obligations. The new economy and social order that emerged in second- and first-century B.C. Italy was marked by the production of a substantial agricultural surplus – and simultaneously shortages and suffering among some Italians and Romans. In the late Empire the introduction of new forms of labour organization (*coloni, laeti,* federates), symbolizing loss of 'entitlement' (Sen's term) among the rural population to the products of agriculture and the pastoral industry, presaged the collapse of the political system.

2. FAMINE IN THE GREEK WORLD

Famine is a subject of vast implications. It has received in recent years a great deal of attention from geographers, demographers, economists and agronomists, and the issues they raise make one aware of the limitations of our knowledge when we look for their counterparts in antiquity and remind us of the relatively small scale of most events that take place on the Greek stage. Definitions of famine, such as 'The archetypal famine extends over a wide area and affects a large population' or '...a protracted total shortage of food in a restricted geographical area, causing widespread disease and death from starvation' make the temporary shortages of grain in the Greek cities of the historical period seem trivial.[1] Whether because of the nature of our sources or a gentler reality, the appalling deathtolls, suffering and degradation of medieval and early modern Europe, and in the much more recent past of neighbouring continents, confront us in the Greek and Roman world almost solely under conditions of siege (e.g. Xen. *Hell.* 2. 2. 11 and 21; Polyb. 1. 84. 9).

It is, however, worth considering whether some of the basic attitudes and institutions dealing with the food supply of Classical and Hellenistic Greece may not have grown out of the universal experience of societies dependent on subsistence agriculture, while their particular character came from the natural and social environment of early Greece. Writing of early modern Europe Braudel says: 'Famine recurred so consistently for centuries on end that it became incorporated into man's biological regime and built into his daily life.'[2] In Greek myth and mythical history, and especially in aetiologies, instances abound of abnormal conditions, usually drought (*auchmos*) when specified, which result in crop failure (*aphoria*) and famine (*limos*). The precipitating causes are violations of social and religious norms and once, with the goddess Demeter's sorrowing for her daughter's rape, a disruption of order among the gods which is resolved by the establishment of the cycle of seasons on their part and of corresponding rituals for mankind.[3] We should see these stories as reflecting the long experience of a culture at the mercy essentially of one crop's success in an often capricious climate and we should not expect to identify specific historical episodes behind them.[4] When we come to our first individual voice in Hesiod's *Works and Days*, *limos* spares the righteous and industrious but, with the like-sounding *loimos*, pestilence, is Zeus's scourge upon a whole community for the wickedness of one man (230, 243, 299). The standard curse attached to formal oaths far into the Hellenistic age echoes Hesiod's language in invoking the sterility of the earth on those who foreswear (e.g. Aeschines 3. 111; *SIG*[3] 120, 85-86). Hesiod's preachment and the formulas of oath both have their source in a view of the interrelation of nature and society, with the failure of the earth to bear fruit as a supreme penalty. In a strikingly traditional passage Thucydides underlines the magnitude of the Peloponnesian War by referring to the exceptional earthquakes, eclipses, droughts, famines and the great plague (1. 23. 3). Polybius distinguishes conditions such as the depopulation of Greece, which he blames on human choice, from natural calamities such as disease and the destruction of crops by bad weather, which are caused by Chance and the Divine and about which it is reasonable to consult oracles and make sacrifices (36. 17). Famine and its causes could not easily be detached from an old, fatalistic view of the world.

In the actual experience of later populations the threat of starvation came at least as much from war, politics and the manipulation of markets as from natural failures, and these last might occur out of sight in remote parts. By then the communities whose problems with food supply come to our attention are those of town-dwellers, depending heavily on imported grain. *sitodeia* ('grain shortage') or an equivalent, rather than *limos* ('hunger', 'starvation', 'famine'), is standard in the many inscriptions referring to emergencies in the food supply from the 4th cent. B.C. on (one example, *sitou endeia*, in the 5th cent., *IG* I³ 30 = I² 31). The grain trade itself is the concern of other contributors. I should like to consider how we may usefully study the continuing dangers to food supply in the Greek world, the hazards, as the ecological anthropologists term them, and the means the Greeks possessed to cope with them, especially in the earlier, formative centuries, when the great majority relied on local sources for their food. This approach may help us to understand what sometimes seem to be partial and contradictory measures in later times. We may also hope to see what famine in the Greek world had in common with the universal phenomenon and how it differed.

Sedentary cereal agriculture, practised by all Greeks and most of those with whom they had contact, could support larger populations on a given area of land than preceding technologies, and grain could be stored with reasonable safety and moved more easily than other available foods. Once established this regime was inescapable, unless a drastic drop in population occurred. But wheat and barley, the chief grains used by the Greeks, are greatly affected by the amount and the timing of rainfall. Between autumn and winter sowing to spring and summer harvesting, according to the most suitable schedule in the climate of the lands bordering the Aegean and Ionian Seas, the crop could be severely reduced by inadequate or inappropriate rainfall.[5] Fluctuation from year to year is unpredictable and so too success in the production of the staple food. The austere Theophrastus twice reports the saying, *etos pherei ouchi aroura*, 'the year, not the soil, determines the yield' (*Hist. Plant.* 8. 7; *Caus. Plant.* 3. 23. 4). Variations resulting in a half, a quarter or a sixth of average annual rainfall are reported in modern observations.[6] One would expect one or two years of each decade to be dangerously low in precipitation.[7] This single criterion of total annual rainfall will miss another serious danger, abnormal distribution of rainfall within a year. Taken together the hazards are seen to be complex.

For most Greek lands drought, not flood, was the chief dread, and without minimizing the devastation drought can cause, we should note that Greeks were usually spared prolonged cold, wet weather, the chief natural cause of famine in more northerly Europe, and the cataclysmic flooding of river valleys which, as in China, breeds disease.[8] Plant diseases and pests, which often accompany excessively wet weather, are mentioned but do not seem to have been as significant for crops as the direct impact of weather.[9] To be sure, concentration on the most suitable and desirable crop brings greater vulnerability to the diseases of that crop and the weeds that flourish with it and reduce the yield. Fallow and especially fallow plowing, by creating an ecological vacuum as it has been called, mitigated these dangers but did so at the cost of reduced arable land, and may have been less of an option for those with the least land who were always closest to starvation.[10]

The geographical distribution of rainfall within the Greek homelands is highly irregular. The shifting of stormtracks may result in a year of light rainfall in one area with a year of normal or heavy rainfall nearby. The many mountains and stretches of sea add further complications.[11] Poor crops from bad weather may thus be a local problem, disastrous to those without access to grain from more fortunate areas but less serious once a grain trade is established. Some areas could be grain exporters or importers depending on conditions, cf. Antigonos's letter to the Teans, mostly concerned with importing grain but touching on exports as well (*SIG*[3] 344 §11). The Selymbrians' law against export of grain indicates that normally they needed all their local production. But once, when there was famine elsewhere and the government was short of cash, sufficient surpluses existed for all grain beyond a year's supply in each individual's possession to be expropriated and then resold to exporters at a profit to the state.[12] Even before the development of a regular grain trade Hesiod allows that for 50 days after the summer solstice, after harvest (and thus after one's own crop has come in and is known to be more than adequate) one may sail with one's surplus, leaving the bulk of one's *bios* at home. One may also sail, though more dangerously, in spring which would be the worst time for those areas which had had a poor harvest the previous summer (*Works and Days* 663-94). The sea makes communication between areas with and without a surplus possible and must be a prime reason for the Greeks' being spared the colossal disasters of large, continental land masses.[13]

But the sea was also the favoured highway for violent seizure. One may wonder how much of the endemic piracy of the Aegean was the work of subsistence farmers seeking to survive in bad years. *leistai* were dangerous, not disreputable, and in later centuries the Athenians did not apologize for *katagein*, the forcible bringing into port of grain ships on the high seas.[14] On land the costs of transport over mountains may have been too great to sustain regular trade in bulk but would not deter a starving man, if the weather had been better on the other side, which, given the nature of the climate, it may well have been. If he had pack animals and something to offer he would endure a disadvantageous exchange to survive.[15] Otherwise he might steal the food source that provided its own transportation. The cattle raids heard of in early poetry are presented as heroic feats (but cf. *Iliad* 3. 10-11). We are rapidly running beyond the evidence, but may not hungry farmers often have echoed the words of Eurylochos persuading the crewmen of Odysseus to slaughter the cattle of the sun: 'to die by starvation is the most pitiful death' (*Odyssey* 12. 342)?

Besides diversity in geography and weather, diversification of the types of food sources between areas and within a given area help to diffuse the risk of famine. The same abnormal weather will not affect grain, fruit trees and flocks to an equal degree, although repeated years of low rainfall will be destructive to all (cf. Hdt. 4. 151, the death of all but one tree on Thera after seven years of drought). Areas that concentrate heavily on one crop are at greatest risk.[16] Diversification is in any case necessary to make the fullest use of the varied Greek landscape. Hedging the risks in this way is a strategy firmly embedded in communities where traditional farming is still practised on the Greek mainland and the despair of rationalizing reformers.[17] It was probably also deeply rooted in the practices of middling to small farmers in antiquity. Obviously the existence of a market greatly increases the feasibility of engaging in the production of foods that are less basic to survival than cereals. One cannot very well live on olives and wine alone, although olive oil is thought to have saved many in Greece in World War II, as an important part of an inadequate diet and as a prized commodity for exchange. The influence of our sources speaking of the supply problems for the cities of the Classical and Hellenistic periods, as well as the fact that in normal times cereals were undoubtedly the staple food, may cause us to neglect other elements in the ancient diet. The fig, for instance, recurs constantly in leases of land and Philip V had to be content with figs to feed his troops in Asia Minor when he could not secure grain (Polyb. 16. 24. 9). The whole subject needs further study. I mention here two further aspects that may be thought of as coping mechanisms.

Most cultures turn to unusual or despised foods in times of shortage. Hesiod's *malache* and *asphodelos* are probably examples.[18] Galen quotes a passage of Hippocrates on the ailments of lentil-eaters and vetch-eaters and adds 'in famine'.[19] Since both were widely cultivated in Classical times either tastes had changed when Galen wrote or, as is quite possible, they were grown primarily for animal fodder. Understandably such famine foods were local, often wild and not items of trade between cities.

Cattle, consuming grain that cannot be stored beyond a year, have been reported as a famine reserve.[20] In Greece, first through aristocratic piety and largesse and later through state policy, animal sacrifice distributed meat to the community. Cattle, less easily moved en masse to seasonal pasture, were at least partly grain-fed; sheep and goats ate lowland grass, the stubble of harvested fields (and sometimes the young grain, to thin it), and most of all the greenery of the largely unarable hills and mountains. Their sustenance, of course, would also be threatened by drought but sheep and goats were not so dependent as grain-eating men on a very limited area. The contribution of animals to the Greek diet in the Classical period was minor but may have been crucial in famine situations.

With the expectation of famine certain but unpredictable what planning could be done to increase the chances of survival? Storage against a bad year was an obvious precaution. Adequate stores are stressed by Hesiod as part of his influential ideal of self-sufficiency (*Works and days* 298 ff., 361 ff.). Ethnographic information on traditional farmers in contemporary Greece suggests that most families overestimate their consumption needs and aim at storing about double that estimate.[21] We have seen that the Selymbrians were once left with only a year's supply for each household, a gamble and not evidently their preferred practice. The protection is thin. I should but do not know how long grain could be stored with safety, but two or three lean years in a row would wipe out the reserves of all but the most provident and wealthy. Communal or state storage would have been more effective, as can be seen vividly in *Genesis* 41. 33-56. One may suspect that the large storage facilities of the Bronze Age palaces of the Aegean helped to provide a cushion that evened out the impact of bad years. But public storage in later Greece is not conspicuous. Grain-storage facilities are mentioned in an inscription of Olbia (*SIG*[3] 495. 145) and an Athenian *strategos* is commended for repairing grain stores in a fort.[22] But the *stoa alphitopolis* in the Peiraeus (Aristoph. *Ekkl.* 685) need have been no more than its name implies, a place for selling barley and perhaps wheat. I dare say I have missed less ambiguous examples but the general impression is likely to remain correct, that storage is essentially the concern of the *oikos* and that public efforts were directed to securing a current supply.[23] For most years that would have been no problem for Athens since with its large demand it offered the most profitable market.[24]

Cult perhaps provides better examples of a communal reserve in the *aparchai*, the first-fruits, in effect a tithe given to the gods. In Athens practical administration and myth were brought to bear on collecting for Demeter and Kore of Eleusis 1/600 of all barley and 1/1200 of all wheat grown in Attica and its possessions, and wishfully perhaps in the other Greek cities as well.[25] By the time we first see the institution in the later 5th cent. the grain is stored in silos built for the purpose and from there sold for cult expenses. In 329/28 B.C. Eleusinian grain is sold at prices fixed by the assembly and therefore, it is supposed, below the current market price.[26] These are years of serious food shortage in Athens. If the practice was old one would suppose that originally the collected grain was first used in the gods' festival, a form of distribution, and then as a reserve to be called on in emergency; famine was at the heart of the cult's founding myth. If there is validity in such speculation it may also be relevant to the Greek custom of borrowing from their sacred treasures, not least the *aparchai* of Athena kept on the Acropolis. The Samian grain law of the 2nd cent. B.C. speaks of purchasing the Goddess's grain, the 1/20 collected from the territory of Anaia, at a price no less than that fixed previously by the *demos*. Thereafter purchase of grain from Anaia may be made if it is advantageous to do so. The Goddess's tithe is a first resource for the city but normally there was concern that her funds be maintained. That might not have been the case in a famine (*SIG*[3] 976, 23-34). These two examples of what looks to be a traditional reserve also show its limitations. It can be drawn only from land over which the cult has a claim, a claim which was widely interpreted by 5th century Athens. By the 4th century territory under Athenian control could supply only a minor part of her needs. It is time to consider how Greek cities reacted to food crises once a significant portion of their food came from abroad.

By the Peloponnesian War at the latest Athens received enough overseas grain to meet its essential needs, for that is the fundamental assumption of Pericles' policy of abandoning the countryside of Attica to the enemy.[27] The conversion of a situation in which it was observed that enough grain came in to feed Athenian stomachs to one in which it was vital for that flow to be maintained is seen in Athens' firm use of military and political force to protect ships carrying grain to Athens and to deny the grain she needed to others. I would suggest that overall Athenian actions were very limited in character, even when we include the fostering of good relations with grain-producing states, notably the Bosporan kingdom in the Pontos, the requirement that residents of Athens may only ship grain to the Peiraeus and that residents may only make maritime loans for voyages bringing grain to Athens.[28] The last two may be thought of as commercial versions of *katagein*, bringing grain ships into harbour. More enterprising ventures seem to be lacking. Were ships ever obtained and manned by the state for the purpose of bringing grain to the city? Is it clear that any Athenian colony, or perhaps any colony, was founded to grow and send back food to the mother city? We see rather a tinkering with a pattern that had developed gradually. To keep up the normal flow was also to maintain access to the main short-term solution to a shortage of local grain. One wonders how large a part domestic production still played not so much its actual proportions, which are beyond us,[29] as in the thinking of the citizens. Generals were still honoured in the 3rd century for ensuring that the local harvest was brought in.[30]

It is more difficult to say for cities other than Athens when interruption of the grain trade became more serious than a failure of local crops. Aigina was surely among the first to find itself in this position and the earliest explicit reference to the grain trade is the story of Xerxes in 480 observing grain ships from the Pontos headed for Aigina and the Peloponnesos (7. 147. 2).[31] The earliest restriction on export may also have been directed against Aigina's appetite. Solon's (Plut. *Sol.* 24. 1) prohibition of the export of any Attic produce except the olive must have been aimed primarily at cereals, the most widely grown produce. Large land-owners presumably found it profitable to send their surpluses abroad to consumers who had more to offer in exchange than did Athenians who were not self-sufficient, and the most obvious market would have been that of Aegina with a population out of proportion to its local resources. Famine is not irrelevant here for it may only have been in bad years that 6th century Athens needed all the grain it produced, but those years are precisely what hastened, if they did not actually cause, the indebtedness and bondage of the poorest in the agricultural population.[32] The economic development of Aigina would inevitably have impinged on its more old-fashioned neighbours.

After the Persian Wars the importation of grain had become so necessary for the city of Teos that public officials were required thrice yearly to curse anyone who interfered with the importation by land or by sea (*SIG*[3] 337-8, Meiggs-Lewis *GHI* 30). Because of the regular repetition the curse has been thought to be a permanent feature of public ritual, not a response to a particular emergency (Meiggs-Lewis *ad loc.*). But we hear of a serious drought that dried up rivers and lakes in Asia Minor in the reign of Artaxerxes (464-24), close enough to the suggested date of the inscription (470) to make it possible that the grain trade is included in a more general curse at a time when dependence on imported grain first became vital.[33] The reference to land as well as sea, if it is not formulaic, reminds us of Antigonos's remarks to the Teans at the end of the 4th century that his crown lands lay nearby and could supply their needs (*SIG*[3] 344, 83-85). With due respect to the continuing power of religion, one must be struck by the Tean reliance on curses while Athens was establishing her muscular control.

Early in the Peloponnesian War Athens gave permission for Methone and Aphytis to import a specified amount of grain 'from Byzantion' (*IG* I[3] 61, 34-41, Meiggs-Lewis *GHI* 65; *IG* I[3] 63, 10-19, *ATL* II, D 21). Evidently the Hellespontophylakes would not normally permit the passage of grain ships without a licence from Athens. Difficulties with the Macedonian king Perdikkas probably prevented Methone from getting her normal supply from the hinterland. The implication of this licensing system is that the majority of the cities of the empire did not have freedom to import grain from the Pontos and that, in one way or another, they could survive without it, from their own resources, from land areas nearby or from elsewhere in the Aegean. Immediate Athenian interests were no doubt the only active considerations when a tight grip was placed on the Hellespont but there is no reason to suppose that the Athenians wished deliberately to weaken their allies or to add unnecessarily to disaffection. Specific hardships could be dealt with by appeal to Athens. For the most part they could manage.[34]

In its time of strength Athens used its power when its wealth was not sufficient to keep quantities of grain coming into the Peiraieus. From the later 4th century and into the Hellenistic and Roman periods throughout the Greek world we hear a great deal about private or privately assisted state actions to secure grain. Private persons, first foreigners and then residents, both citizens and metics, either furnish free grain or grain at the normal price at a time of shortage and high prices, or provide loans without interest or at a low interest for the purchase of grain (*sitonia*). Officials are appointed, *sitonai*, grain-purchasers, who may themselves make generous contributions. Subscriptions (*epidoseis*) are raised from the more affluent to provide funds for the purchases. City funds, at a time when they were less substantial than the resources of wealthy individuals, may have been committed reluctantly.[35]

We hear of most of these arrangements in emergencies and it is doubtful that they operated in many cities year in and year out.[36] We have no idea how long the impressive mechanism of the Samian grain law was actually in effect. No more than the public distributions and sales of the Classical period did these later benefactions, dependent on the wealth and good will of individuals, constitute a system designed to meet the cities' needs.[37] They are part of the pattern of social gestures, gaining credit for the benefactors and directed both to pressing needs, such as military defence and the food supply, and to more distinctly symbolic, not practical ends in the religious sphere. The organized subscriptions were directed to cult and to emergency military expenses more often than to the food supply. Gifts of grain were distributed among all the citizens, even as at a festival the participants shared equally, aside from honours for specified officials, in all the food furnished. The beneficiaries are never explicitly described as the needy before the Roman period (*IG* IV 2, 11-14) except by Theophrastus's boaster (*Char.* 23. 5).[38] As in cult outsiders might be excluded – the gift of the Egyptian Psamettichos in 445/44 resulted in a scrutiny of the citizen rolls.[39] The model for public generosity in Greece may well have been the cult feast, an opportunity for wealth to be used to gain honour for its possessors. In the late Archaic and the Classical periods private wealth was exploited for political purposes[40] and then harnessed by the city in the form of liturgies. As it reappears in the Hellenistic period it is more an instrument for the social advancement of the rich than a reliable resource for the community.[41] In a crisis the leaders of the community, themselves among the affluent, could set an example, initiate a subscription and hope for the help of those who disposed of much money or grain. The great benefactor regains the dimensions of a mythical hero: Erechtheus becomes an Egyptian resident in Athens who, at a time of great drought and crop failure everywhere except Egypt, is able through his Egyptian ties to convey grain to Athens from Egypt and is rewarded as *euergetes* with the kingship, and introduces the rites of Demeter to Eleusis (Diod. Sic. 1. 29. 1).

I conclude with the admission of a paradox. Despite the deep-seated fear of famine and familiarity with it, the Greek cities developed very limited strategies to confront the danger. Some of the risks, I have suggested, were blunted by the geographical and ecological conditions. Reliance on the ability of the individual *oikos* to cope and survive remained strong in a world where town and country largely interpenetrated. In emergencies certain institutions, still with a decided cultic flavour, could be turned to. We should also allow for the predominance of short-term views and perhaps a tendency to remember and to act on the basis of happier experiences.[42] Gernet, whose work remains supremely enlightening, said of Athens 'on n'était pas fait à l'adversité'. I suspect the same might have been said of most Greek cities.[43]

Stanford

MICHAEL JAMESON

MICHAEL JAMESON

NOTES

1. Citations from M. K. Bennett, 'Famine', *Intern. Encycl. Soc. Sc.* (1968) 322; W. A. Dando, *The geography of famine* (1980) 65.

2. F. Braudel, *Capitalism and material life 1400-1800* (1973) 38.

3. E.g. Diod. Sic. 4.61, Porph. *de abst.* 2.29-30; *Hymn to Dem.* 302-13.

4. Cf. J. McK. Camp, *The water supply of ancient Athens from 3000 to 86 B.C.* Diss. Princeton (1977), and 'A drought in the late eighth century B.C.', *Hesperia* 48 (1979) 397-411, for ambitious attempts to detect major periods of drought with long term effects in Athens in the late 8th and late 4th centuries B.C. The subject deserves discussion along with the late Bronze Age drought of R. Carpenter, *Discontinuity in Greek civilization* (1968). Only the 4th century drought is satisfactorily established; see the treatment of the historical evidence in S. Isager, M. H. Hansen, *Aspects of Athenian society in the fourth century B.C.* (1975) 204-6.

5. Theophr. *Hist. Plant.* 8.6.5; Hes. *Works and Days* 468 ff., to cite only ancient sources. The insignificance of irrigation is also noteworthy.

6. A. Philippson, *Das Klima Griechenlands* (1948) 113.

7. H. A. Forbes, *Strategies and soils: technology, production and environment in the peninsula of Methana.* Diss. Pennsylvania (1982) 303-14.

8. W. H. McNeill, *Plagues and peoples* (1976) 76-80, 122 on the Yangtze valley. Unlike the Egyptians, the Greeks knew of only one flood, Plato, *Tim.*23B (*contra*, Schol. on 22A).

9. This estimate of their relative significance is, to be sure, based on impressions. There is no lack of reference to rusts and pests in Theophrastus, e.g. *Caus. Plant.* 3.22.2, 4.14; *Hist. Plant.* 8.10, and severe and prolonged winters were remembered and were certainly damaging.

10. W. H. McNeill, *The human condition. An ecological and historical view* (1980), esp. 15-6.

11. Arist. *Met.* 2.4.360B5-13; Philippson (n. 6) 112-5; H. H. Lamb, *Climate: present, past and future. II. Climate history and the future* (1977) 421.

12. [Arist.] *Econ.* 2.2.17.1348B33-139A2. On the textual problem, B. A. van Groningen, *Aristote. Le seconde libre de l'Économique* (1933) 118-9.

13. Cf. [Xen.]Ath.Pol. 2.6: 'Land-powers are hard hit by crop failures that come from Zeus, sea-powers can bear them easily. For not all the land is affected at the same time, so food comes to the rulers of the sea from lands that are flourishing'.

14. G. E. M. de Ste Croix, *The origins of the Peloponnesian War* (1972) 314.

15. Cf. the efforts of Phleious in wartime, Xen. *Hell.* 7.2.17.

16. Cf. E. A. Wrigley, *Population and history* (1969) 66-8 for resistance to famine in adjoining areas of N. France.

17. H. A. Forbes (n. 7) 263-318; '"We have a little of everything", the ecological basis of some agricultural practices in Methana, Trizinia', *Regional variation in modern Greece and Cyprus: toward a perspective on the ethnography of Greece*, M. Dimen, E. Friedl (edd.) (1976) 236-50.

18. *Works and Days* 41, cf. Aristoph. *Plut.* 544; Galen, *Alim.fac.* 2.63 (*CMG* 5.4.2, 325).

19. Hippocr. *Epid.* 2.4.3 = 6.4.11; Galen, *Alim. fac.* 1.29 (*CMG* 257); and on acorns in famine, 2.38.5 (*CMG* 305). Cf. G. E. M. de Ste Croix, *The Class struggle in the ancient Greek world* (1981) 14. Ethnographic evidence in Mary Forbes, 'Gathering in the Argolid: a subsistence subsystem in a Greek agricultural community', *Regional variation* (n. 17) 251-64.

20. R. and N. Dyson Hudson in *African food production systems*, P. F. M. McLoughlin (ed.) (1970) 91-123, cited by R. McC.Netting, 'Agrarian ecology', *Ann. Rev. of Anthr.* 3 (1974) 44.

21. L. Foxhall, H. A. Forbes, 'Σιτομετρεία; the role of grain as a staple food in classical antiquity', *Chiron* 12 (1982) 41-90, at 57 n. 2 and 68 n. 95; Forbes (n. 7) 303-14. De Ste Croix (n. 19) 221 cites Auson. *de hered.* 27-8 for always laying in two years' supply of produce.

22. *IG* II² 1281 in Fr. G. Maier, *Griechische Mauerbauinschriften* I (1959) 117, who shows the reference is to the fort, not a village.

23. The Samian grain law provides for grain to be distributed monthly until it is used up: *SIG*³ 976, 56-7.

24. H. Francotte, 'Le pain à bon marché et le pain gratuit dans les cités grecques', *Mél. Nicole* (1910) 136-7.

25. *IG* I³ 78 = I² 76, Meiggs-Lewis, *GHI* 73; *IG* II² 140; 1672, 263-96; 2956-7.

26. *IG* II² 1672, 263-96.

27. On the actual damage done by enemy ravaging, which has been exaggerated, see V. D. Hanson, *Warfare and agriculture in ancient Greece* (1983). Continual warfare could leave the land unworked and unsown, e.g. *IG* II² 834, 8 (*SIG*³ 497).

28. Useful accounts of Athenian practice are in L. Gernet, 'L'approvisionnement d'Athènes en blé au Ve et au IVe siècle', *Mél. hist. anc.* (1909) 271-391; Isager, Hansen (n. 4) 19-29; R. J. Hopper, *Trade and industry in classical Greece* (1979) 71-92.

29. Cf. Gernet (n. 28) 293-6; A. Jardé, *Les céréales dans l'antiquité grecque. I. La production* (1925) 36-57; Isager, Hansen (n. 4) 11-9.

30. E.g. *IG* II² 682, 35-6, and T. L. Shear, *Kallias of Sphettos and the revolt of Athens in 286 B.C.* Hesperia Suppl. 17 (1978) 20-1.

31. T. J. Figuerra, *Aegina. Society and politics* (1981) on Aegina's early economy (p. 234 on the Peloponnesos here).

32. On the island of Amorgos I have been told that in the past many small farmers lost their property and put themselves or their children into virtual slavery to large landowners when bad seasons wiped out their reserves. The principle is clear enough and nothing is proved for antiquity.

33. For the drought, Str. 1.3.4. If it occurred in the reign of Artaxerxes I it fits the date 480-50 B.C., later rather than earlier, for the Tean curses favoured by P. Hermann, *Chiron* 11 (1981) 6.

34. On the Athenian control of the sea and its use to hurt her enemies, M. I. Finley, 'The fifth-century Athenian empire: a balance sheet', *Imperialism in the ancient world*, P. Garnsey, C. R. Whittaker (edd.) (1978) 118-21. In the Peloponnesian War, Athens' aims in Sicily are spoken of in terms of denying grain to the Peloponnesos, not of securing it for herself (Thuc. 3.86.4).

35. Antigonos denies the Tean request to raise their grain fund above 1400 staters (*SIG*³ 344 §10). On the various Hellenistic devices see Francotte (n. 24); A. R. Hands, *Charities and social aid in Greece and Rome* (1968) 89-110; J. Triantaphyllopoulos, 'Παράπρασις', *Acta of the Fifth Epigr. Congr. 1967* (1971) 65-9.

36. *IG* V 2.268 (Hands (n. 35) 189) of the late 1st cent. B.C. records the establishment of a fund for supplying grain in perpetuity. But it stands alone. An inscription of Iasos grandly proclaims that the *demos* should forever live happily on a plenitude of grain, a hope based on *epidoseis*, A. Wilhelm, 'Σιτομετρεία', *Mél. Glotz* (1932) 899-908.

37. Gernet (n. 28) 375-85; P. Veyne, *Le pain et le cirque* (1976) 209-28.

38. By congratulating himself on his generosity the boaster defines himself as *patronus* to *clientelae* and thus separates himself from the community as a whole. When in the Hellenistic period we find distributions or subsidized sales being made available to slaves and foreigners, we see that a different community is being recognized. Instead of a theoretically undifferentiated group of citizens who are the agents *and* the beneficiaries, there is on one side the elite and on the other all the population of the community whose survival and docility are regarded as desirable.

39. Philoch. *FGrH* 328F119, Schol. Aristoph. *Wasps* 718, Plut. *Per.* 37.4. It is not clear whether there was a famine at the time, despite one of the scholia in the Venetus ms. of the *Wasps*; cf. J. Labarbe, 'La distribution de blé de 445/4 à Athènes et ses incidences démographiques', *Sozialökon. Verhältn. Alt. Or. u. Klass. Alt.* (1961) 106-18. A *sitodeia* is given as the reason for *xenelasia* (the driving out and thus creating of the *perioikoi* at Sparta), Theop. *FGrH* 115F178.

40. J. K. Davies, *Wealth and the power of wealth in classical Athens* (1981).

41. Francotte (n. 24) 148-9 saw an inescapable slide from emergency distributions to the poor to routine insistence on free grain, and woe betide the rich who failed to subscribe. I see nothing to support this view.

42. Cf. A. V. Kirkby, 'Individual and community responses to rainfall variability in Oaxaca, Mexico', *Natural hazards: local, national, global*, G. F. White (ed.) (1974).

43. Gernet (n. 28) 378. I am uncomfortably aware of what has been omitted in these pages, especially any consideration of long-term consequences of famine, such as emigration, and the relationship of disease to famine (I think they are alternatives for the Greeks and are hardly ever attested together, despite what we might expect, another reason perhaps for the relative mildness of Greek famine). I have benefited from conversation and bibliographical help from William Skinner, David Sahlin, and Pan Yotopoulos, but they may be surprised at the results.

3. LE COMMERCE DES CÉRÉALES CHEZ LES GRECS DE L'ÉPOQUE ARCHAÏQUE

Y a-t-il eu, chez les Grecs de l'époque archaïque, un commerce des produits de base, et notamment des céréales? Depuis quand? Quelle était son importance quantitative et quel était son rôle dans l'ensemble de la vie sociale? Malgré la pauvreté décourageante de notre documentation, il n'est peut-être pas téméraire de tenter, après d'autres,[1] de répondre à ces questions.

Aux VIIIᵉ et VIIᵉ siècles, on le sait, les Grecs entretenaient des rapports commerciaux intenses avec les habitants de la Syrie du Nord – où aboutissait la principale route commerciale entre la Mésopotamie et la Méditerranée.[2] Les établissements gréco-phéniciens d'Al Mina et de Tell Sukas étaient certainement deux parmi les points d'où partaient vers l'Egée les produits artisanaux de luxe, d'origine phénicienne, syrienne, mésopotamienne, ourartienne, que les fouilles ont mis au jour en pays grec. Avec quoi les Grecs payaient-ils ces produits? Les vases grecs peints de cette époque qui ont été trouvés au Proche Orient en dehors des établissements mentionnés, ne sont pas très nombreux.[3] D'autre part, nous savons qu'en dehors de la poterie, la technique grecque était, à cette époque, inférieure à celles des civilisations orientales. Il faut donc supposer que les Grecs vendaient surtout des esclaves et des produits agricoles: huile d'olive[4] (servant entre autres à la production de parfums), vin et – du moins lorsqu'il s'agissait de rapports avec des Phéniciens – céréales.[5] Dans l'*Odyssée* 15.403-84, nous voyons des marchands phéniciens vendre des objets de luxe (*athurmata*) et acheter de la nourriture (*biotos*), c'est-à-dire, sans doute, essentiellement des grains. Etant donné l'existence des établissements d'Al Mina et de Tell Sukas, il est raisonnable de penser que des marchands grecs, aux VIIIᵉ-VIIᵉ siècles, faisaient l'inverse, c'est-à-dire allaient au Proche Orient vendre du *biotos* et acheter des *athurmata*.[6] Cela est d'autant plus probable que la terminologie du commerce que l'*Odyssée* et les *Travaux* d'Hésiode nous font, directement ou indirectement, connaître et dont je traite ou traiterai ailleurs[7] (*phorton agein, phortizesthai, hode, hodaia, empole, empolan, emporos, emporie, prekter*), témoigne qu'à l'époque où ces poèmes ont été composés, le commerce maritime, en tant qu'activité spécialisée et professionnelle, était exercé par des Grecs depuis longtemps. Remarquons aussi qu'en *Iliade* 9.71-2 ce sont des 'navires des Achéens' qui transportent tous les jours du vin de la Thrace à l'armée qui assiège Troie (cf. *Iliade* 7.467-75).

Dans les *Travaux* d'Hésiode, 618-94, nous constatons que des propriétaires de terre moyens exercent parfois le commerce maritime: ils transportent outre-mer une partie de leur *bios*, c'est-à-dire des denrées, essentiellement des céréales (cf. 31-2 et 42) produites sur leurs biens. Si des propriétaires de terre moyens vendaient des céréales à l'étranger, il est permis de supposer que les grands propriétaires de terre en vendaient beaucoup plus et plus souvent; seulement, ils ne voyageaient sans doute pas eux-mêmes pour les vendre (cf. ci-dessous, 24).

L'*Odyssée* témoigne d'autre part que les Grecs, non seulement vendaient des grains, mais en achetaient aussi. En 17.248-50, le chevrier Mélanthios dit, en se référant au porcher Eumée: 'Je le transporterai un jour, sur un navire noir aux beaux bancs, loin d'Ithaque, pour qu'il me fasse gagner beaucoup de nourriture (*biotos*)'. Certes, on ne voit pas comment un esclave chevrier pourrait aller outre-mer faire du commerce. Mélanthios parle à tort et à travers; on dirait qu'il applique mécaniquement un schéma banal de pensée et d'expression, d'autant plus que ses propos ressemblent un peu à ceux que prononce l'un des prétendants en *Odyssée* 20. 381-83 ('jetons ces étrangers dans un navire aux nombreux bancs et transportons-les chez les Sicèles, d'où cela te ferait gagner un prix convenable'). Mais cette constatation ne fait que rendre ce passage plus significatif: il en ressort qu'aller outre-mer vendre des esclaves et acheter des céréales est une chose normale dans la société où vit le poète de l'*Odyssée*.

Ce témoignage de l'*Odyssée* renforce une conclusion qu'on peut tirer, qu'on a souvent tirée[8] des données archéologiques concernant les colonies grecques de Sicile: les grandes quantités de vases peints de la seconde moitié du VIIIe siècle et du VIIe siècle, fabriqués à Corinthe ou dans d'autres villes de la Grèce et qu'on a trouvés en Sicile, prouvent, quoique de manière indirecte, que le commerce des céréales siciliennes, attesté à l'époque classique, a commencé aussitôt après la fondation des colonies grecques dans cette île. Il est en effet très probable que ce sont surtout des céréales qui constituaient la contre-partie de ces marchandises.

Qu'en est-il du commerce des céréales égyptiennes? Le témoignage le plus ancien sur ce commerce est fourni par un *egkomion* de Bacchylide (fr. 20 B Snell-Maehler), écrit en l'honneur d'Alexandre fils d'Amyntas, roi de Macédoine. Ce poème parle entre autres des rêveries que suscite l'ivresse: la 'douce violence' du vin 'envoie très haut les pensées des hommes'; l'homme ivre 'défait aussitôt les créneaux des villes et croit qu'il exercera le pouvoir autocratique (*monarkhesein*) sur tous les hommes; la maison resplendit d'or et d'ivoire, et des navires porteurs de froment transportent de l'Egypte, sur la mer éblouissante, une grande richesse: c'est ainsi que s'élance le coeur du buveur'. Il est probable que ce poème n'est pas antérieur aux guerres médiques, car le rêve d'un pouvoir universel semble supposer l'expérience de la politique du Grand Roi.[9] Les 'navires porteurs de froment' arrivant de l'Egypte sont-ils une nouveauté de l'époque des guerres médiques? Je ne le pense pas.[10]

Les marchands grecs qui, depuis la fin du VIIe siècle, fréquentaient Naukratis, exportaient en Egypte sans doute du bois, des métaux ou des objets en métal (notamment de l'argent), de l'huile, du vin (pour le vin, voir ce que Strabon 17. 808, dit du frère de Sappho: il se peut que cette information ait été tirée d'un poème de Sappho), peut-être aussi des tissus raffinés de laine. Ils en importaient sans doute des produits artisanaux, spécialités de l'Egypte: papyrus, tissus raffinés de lin, médicaments, objets en verre ou en faïence; mais il faut bien supposer qu'ils importaient également des céréales, car celles-ci étaient, en Egypte, plus abondantes que dans n'importe quelle autre région fréquentée par des marchands grecs. Si on supposait qu'ils n'achetaient que les produits artisanaux mentionnés, il faudrait supposer également qu'ils étaient obligés d'embarquer du lest; mais à quoi bon transporter du sable ou des pierres, alors qu'on peut acheter des céréales bon marché pour les vendre ailleurs beaucoup plus cher?

De même que la Sicile et l'Egypte, la côte septentrionale de la mer Noire était, à l'époque classique, une région d'où les Grecs de Grèce et d'Asie Mineure importaient des céréales. Depuis quand le commerce des céréales pontiques existait-il? Plusieurs savants pensent qu'il n'a commencé qu'au Ve siècle ou dans la seconde moitié du VIe; mais cette opinion me paraît fausse. Elle s'appuie essentiellement sur le fait que pour la période antérieure au milieu du VIe siècle, on ne connaît pas d'indices sérieux de l'existence d'un commerce entre les établissements grecs de la côte septentrionale de la mer Noire et les barbares de l'intérieur, si ce n'est un petit groupe de vases grecs de luxe trouvés à Nemirov, à peu de distance du cours supérieur du Boug méridional.[11] Mais ce fait prouve seulement que les barbares de l'intérieur ne fournissaient pas de céréales aux colonies grecques de la côte. D'ailleurs, pour ce qui concerne les barbares de la steppe ukrainienne, il va de soi qu'ils ne fournissaient pas de céréales, car dans cette région, pendant la période qui va du milieu du VIIe à la fin du VIe siècle, il n'y a pas de traces de population sédentaire.[12] Il faut se demander si les colonies grecques elles-mêmes ne produisaient pas assez de céréales pour pouvoir en vendre aux Grecs des villes de l'Egée. Cela apparaîtra non seulement possible, mais probable, si l'on accepte l'hypothèse de V. V. Lapin,[13] selon laquelle les établissements grecs de la côte septentrionale de la mer Noire auraient été fondés, non pas par des marchands, ainsi qu'on l'a soutenu pendant longtemps, mais par des gens qui cherchaient de la terre à cultiver, et auraient été, au point de vue économique, des colonies de caractère productif, avant tout agricole, analogues à celles que les Grecs ont fondées en Occident. Certains éléments de la construction de Lapin ne résistent pas à la critique, mais dans l'ensemble, Lapin a sans doute raison. Une fois admis que la plupart des habitants de ces colonies, à l'époque archaïque, tiraient leur nourriture de leur territoire civique ainsi que des eaux des environs, nous devrons en venir à la conclusion[14] que c'est en grande partie avec de la nourriture qu'ils achetaient la céramique peinte et d'autres produits artisanaux provenant des villes de l'Egée et qu'on trouve dans le sol de ces colonies.[15] La nourriture qu'ils avaient à vendre, c'était du poisson salé, car les eaux des fleuves et de la mer de cette région étaient bien plus riches en poissons que celles de l'Egée, et il y avait sur place des salines naturelles; c'était en outre et surtout des céréales, car le sol de cette région était extrêmement favorable à la céréaliculture.

Au sujet du commerce du blé pontique, on cite souvent un passage d'Hérodote (7.

147. 2-3), qui raconte qu'étant à Abydos, Xerxès vit des navires porteurs de blé,
provenant du Pont-Euxin et dirigés vers Egine et le Péloponnèse. Il s'agit
certainement d'une anecdote inventée (car le récit se termine par un bon mot), mais
cette invention suppose l'existence d'un commerce du blé provenant de la mer
Noire. Il est vraisemblable que l'anecdote n'est pas née longtemps après l'expédition
de Xerxès. Elle peut donc effectivement témoigner de l'existence d'un commerce du
blé pontique vers la fin de l'époque archaïque.

Evidemment, aussi longtemps que les céréales qui pouvaient être exportées des
colonies grecques de la côte septentrionale de la mer Noire n'ont été produites que
dans leurs territoires, il ne pouvait jamais s'agir de très grandes quantités. Ce n'est
que lorsqu'une partie des barbares de l'arrière-pays ont commencé à produire et à
vendre des céréales, que des quantités considérables de ce produit ont pu être
disponibles dans les ports de cette région. (Au temps d'Hérodote, non loin du
territoire d'Olbia-Borysthénès, il y avait les Kallippidai, mi-Grecs, mi-Scythes, qui
cultivaient et mangeaient les céréales, puis les 'Scythes laboureurs', qui cultivaient
les céréales, mais seulement pour les vendre, enfin les 'Scythes agriculteurs'; le reste
des barbares, c'étaient des nomades. Voir Hérodote, 4. 17-18.) Je pense cependant
que les modestes surplus de céréales dont pouvaient disposer les Grecs de cette
région dans la seconde moitié du VIIe et au VIe siècle, étaient suffisants pour rendre
possible un commerce de ce produit. Les agriculteurs à qui Hésiode s'adresse ne
disposent certainement que de modestes surplus de *bios*, et pourtant, il vaut la peine
pour eux d'aller les vendre outre-mer.

On dit souvent que l'importation de céréales en Grèce n'a pu commencer qu'à une
époque où, dans certaines cités, il existait un *demos* urbain nombreux, donc au Ve
siècle ou, au plus tôt, vers le milieu du VIe ou vers la fin du VIIe.[16] Cette opinion ne
tient pas compte des témoignages de l'*Odyssée* et d'Hésiode. Elle ne tient pas
compte non plus des disettes, causées par les caprices du climat, et qui ont dû être
fréquentes et frapper tantôt un territoire, tantôt un autre.[17] Ce n'est, sans doute, que
dans les années excellentes ou moyennes que la production agricole du territoire
d'une cité était suffisante pour nourrir sa population. L'*Odyssée* 15. 404-11,
mentionne un pays 'riche en vaches, en moutons, en vin, en froment', et où 'la
famine n'entre jamais': c'est l'île Syrie; mais dans cette île, il n'y a pas non plus de
maladies: il s'agit donc de 'fairyland'. Le danger de la faim est toujours présent dans
le milieu social auquel s'adressent les *Travaux* d'Hésiode, et qui est un milieu de
propriétaires de terre moyens.

Outre les disettes dues aux caprices du climat, il y avait les ravages que causaient
les guerres fréquentes. Dévaster les récoltes de l'ennemi, c'était une pratique
normale, dans ces guerres qui se combattaient dans la saison d'été.

Hérodote raconte (1. 17-22) que sous les règnes de Sadyatte et d'Alyatte, les
Lydiens firent la guerre aux Milésiens pendant douze ans, et que chaque année, ils
dévastaient les champs de leurs ennemis. Il dit aussi qu'ils n'assiégeaient pas la ville
de Milet, parce que cela ne valait pas la peine, les Milésiens étant maîtres de la mer.

De ce récit, il ressort – ainsi que d'autres l'ont déjà remarqué – que vers la fin du VIIe siècle, les Milésiens étaient en mesure d'importer assez de céréales pour pouvoir faire face à la *sitodeie*. Certes, une guerre aussi longue que celle dont Hérodote parle ici, était tout à fait exceptionnelle; mais une guerre durant une seule saison pouvait suffire à causer une disette.

Ce n'est pas la croissance du *demos* urbain qui a fait naître le commerce des céréales, mais la fréquence des mauvaises récoltes.

Une loi appartenant au premier *axon* des lois de Solon et citée par Plutarque (*Solon* 24) interdit de vendre à des étrangers (*xenoi*) des produits agricoles autres que l'huile; elle ordonne en outre ce qui suit: 'l'archonte prononcera des imprécations (*arai*) contre ceux qui exportent (ces produits), ou alors il payera au trésor public cent drachmes à titre d'amende'.[18] De cette loi, nous pouvons tirer les conclusions suivantes: 1) Les riches propriétaires de terre athéniens du temps de Solon exportaient parfois – sans doute dans les bonnes années – des céréales vers des cités grecques (car les *xenoi* sont normalement des Grecs d'autres cités, non pas des barbares).[19] 2) Cette exportation était contraire aux intérêts de la communauté athénienne; cela permet de supposer que dans l'Attique de cette époque, la production de céréales n'était jamais très abondante, et que l'exportation avait pour conséquence de rendre les céréales plus chères pour ceux parmi les habitants de l'Attique qui étaient obligés, même dans les bonnes années, d'en acheter. 3) Si, en Attique, les céréales n'étaient pas très abondantes dans les bonnes années, il est vraisemblable que dans les mauvaises anées, on en importait de l'étranger. 4) La production d'huile d'olive était assez abondante pour qu'on pût en exporter sans que cela eût des conséquences fâcheuses pour ceux parmi les habitants de l'Attique qui étaient obligés d'en acheter.

Selon Ed. Will,[20] cette loi 'encourageait en fait l'oléiculture en détournant des céréales les derniers producteurs excédentaires, désormais contraints de vendre en Attique où [...] l'importation devait tendre à faire baisser la valeur du blé'. Que la loi ait eu pour conséquence une certaine réduction de la céréaliculture et une certaine extension de l'oléiculture en Attique, est extrêmement vraisemblable. Mais la dernière partie du raisonnement d'Ed. Will me paraît douteuse. Nous ne savons pas, en effet, si en Attique au temps de Solon, on importait beaucoup de céréales dans les bonnes années. Il se peut qu'on n'en importât beaucoup que dans les mauvaises années. Or, dans ces années, malgré l'importation, la valeur des céréales en Attique était sans doute assez élevée pour que les grands propriétaires pussent en vendre avec profit, si tant est qu'ils eussent des excédents à vendre (voir *infra*, p. 23-4). A part cela, je suppose que dans les bonnes années, avant la loi de Solon, les excédents de la production céréalière attique n'étaient pas très importants, car beaucoup de terres de ce pays n'étaient pas bonnes pour les céréales. Je pense donc qu'il faut se garder d'exagérer la portée des changements produits par cette loi de Solon dans l'agriculture attique.

Il convient de préciser – et sur ce point, je suppose qu'Ed. Will serait d'accord –

que, si la loi en question a eu pour conséquence une certaine extension de l'oléiculture attique, ce n'était sans doute pas là le but poursuivi par Solon: il est vraisemblable que le seul but que se proposait le législateur, c'était de protéger les intérêts des acheteurs de produits agricoles.

Ed. Will a écrit en outre:[21] '...la loi solonienne implique un déséquilibre entre la production de l'huile et celle des autres denrées, et cet excès implique à son tour que l'oléiculture s'était développée aux dépens des autres cultures vivrières. Essor qui ne pouvait guère être le fait de l'exploitation paysanne, laquelle ne disposait ni de la superficie, ni, sans doute, des délais nécessaires. On ne se trompera donc pas en imputant le développement exagéré de l'oléiculture à la grande propriété aristocratique. Or l'expansion de l'oliveraie attique est sans doute déjà en elle-même une conséquence de la crise paysanne, car on peut penser que les terres plantées en oliviers furent, dans une large mesure, des tenures paysannes accaparées par le jeu des créances analysé ci-dessus'. – Ce qu'Ed. Will soutient là est une construction hypothétique admissible, mais que rien n'oblige à admettre. En particulier, il n'est nullement évident que les 'exploitations paysannes', dans l'Attique du VIIe ou du début du VIe siècle, n'aient disposé ni de la superficie, ni des délais nécessaires pour la production d'huile pour la vente. Si l'on suppose que ces 'exploitations' étaient des propriétés semblables à celles qu'envisage Hésiode dans les *Travaux*, on admettra que beaucoup d'entre elles pouvaient fort bien, dans les bonnes années, produire des denrées excédentaires, susceptibles d'être vendues. En effet, le propriétaire-type auquel Hésiode s'adresse, est, d'un côté, menacé par la faim et les dettes, mais, de l'autre côté, il a également des chances de prospérer, voire de devenir riche et d'atteindre ainsi l'*arete* et le *kudos*, l'excellence et le prestige éclatant. Il possède un ou deux boeufs et quelques esclaves, il engage, pour les grands travaux, un ouvrier agricole; il possède en outre un bateau et il fait du commerce en exportant une partie du *bios* qu'il a produit. En Béotie, la terre se prête fort bien à la céréaliculture, et c'est sans doute surtout des excédents de céréales qu'on pouvait y obtenir dans les bonnes années. En Attique, une partie des terres (celles des coteaux) sont bonnes pour l'olivier, moins bonnes, voire décidément mauvaises pour les céréales; il est donc permis de supposer que les propriétaires – les petits tout comme les grands – ont misé, de très bonne heure, surtout sur la production d'huile pour obtenir des excédents pour la vente. Bien entendu, la culture principale, en Attique aussi, était celle des céréales; mais il s'agit de voir quelle était la culture qui avait le plus de chances de fournir des excédents.

On rapprochera cette loi solonienne d'une inscription de Téos, Meiggs-Lewis, *GHI* 30 (voir aussi l'édition dans *Sylloge*^{3} 37-8), qui n'est probablement pas de beaucoup postérieure aux guerres médiques. Cette inscription contient une imprécation (*epare*) que les *timoukhoi* sont tenus de prononcer publiquement trois fois par an (s'ils ne le font pas, il seront eux-mêmes sujets à l'imprécation) contre ceux qui commettraient tel ou tel délit. Le texte dit entre autres: 'Si quelqu'un empêche, de quelque manière que ce soit, d'importer des céréales dans le territoire de Téos par mer ou par voie de terre, ou repousse (hors du territoire de Téos) des céréales importées, qu'il périsse, lui-même et sa famille'.[22] Il n'est pas difficile d'imaginer la situation que ce passage du texte envisage: il prévoit le cas où des habitants de Téos, désirant vendre ou prêter des céréales aux conditions les plus avantageuses pour eux, empêcheraient des gens transportant des céreales par mer ou par voie de terre, d'introduire leurs chargements dans le territoire de la cité, ou contraindraient ceux qui l'auraient fait, à repartir avec leurs chargements. Evidemment, il s'agit de nobles riches et puissants, disposant de moyens de contrainte physique suffisants pour empêcher l'importation de céréales étrangères, qui aurait pour conséquence de diminuer la rareté des céréales à Téos et l'avantage qu'ils entendent en tirer. (Bien entendu, ils ne redoutent pas une 'mévente': ce danger n'existe pas.) Leur comportement est tellement nuisible aux intérêts de la communauté, que celle-ci décide de faire prononcer à des magistrats une imprécation contre eux trois fois par an. Remarquons que Téos n'était pas une grande ville.

Il est en somme certain que les cités grecques archaïques ne se nourrissaient pas toujours exclusivement des produits de leurs territoires respectifs. Il reste à voir quels groupes sociaux étaient économiquement en mesure d'acheter des céréales étrangères pour des buts autres que le commerce de gros, et à quels groupes sociaux appartenaient les hommes qui exerçaient le commerce maritime des céréales. (Laissons de côté le commerce par voie de terre, certainement beaucoup moins important.)

La première question renvoie évidemment à une question plus large: quels étaient les groupes sociaux qui achetaient des céréales en général (indigènes ou étrangères) pour des buts autres que le commerce de gros? Pour répondre à cette question, on peut s'appuyer sur un témoignage indirect. En *Odyssée* 14. 323-26, il est question des richesses qu'Ulysse a amassées: 'du bronze, de l'or, du fer très travaillé'. Ces richesses – est-il dit – 'suffiraient à nourrir quelqu'un d'autre [*heteron g'* : c'est-à-dire un homme qui ne soit pas un *basileus* comme Ulysse, mais de condition plus modeste] même jusqu'à la dixième génération'. Cela suppose que dans la société où le poète vit, il y ait des hommes de condition relativement modeste (mais pas basse), qui achètent de la nourriture en la payant avec des objets en bronze, en or ou en fer. Mais c'est là, à ma connaissance, le seul témoignage disponible. Pour l'essentiel, il nous faut raisonner d'après la vraisemblance. Les artisans libres, pas très nombreux, achetaient certainement tous les ans, en contre-partie de leurs produits, toute ou une partie[23] de la nourriture nécessaire à leurs familles et – s'ils en possédaient – à leurs esclaves. Dans les mauvaises années, les propriétaires de terre moyens achetaient sans doute des céréales, en les payant avec du bétail et des esclaves, ou avec des métaux ou des objets artisanaux achetés dans les bonnes années ou pillés au cours de guerres ou de razzias. Il est probable que les grands propriétaires de terre, autrement dit les nobles riches et puissants, achetaient parfois, eux aussi, des céréales.[24] En effet, dans les mauvaises années, le produit de leurs terres pouvait ne pas toujours suffire à nourrir leur famille, leurs chevaux, mulets et ânes ainsi que les gens qui dépendaient d'eux et travaillaient pour eux. Et même s'il suffisait à cela, les grands propriétaires pouvaient avoir besoin de quantités supplémentaires de céréales pour en vendre ou en prêter à des propriétaires de terre moins riches ou à des artisans libres (souvenons-nous du rôle essentiel que jouaient les prêts dans les sociétés grecques archaïques; ces prêts étaient vraisemblablement pour la plupart des prêts de blé), peut-être aussi pour faire des dons susceptibles de créer ou d'entretenir des liens de clientèle politique.

Quant à la seconde question, celle qui concerne les assises sociales du commerce maritime, je crois pouvoir utiliser une construction hypothétique que j'ai proposée ailleurs[25] et qui peut s'appuyer sur quelques indices. Le commerce maritime était en grande partie aux mains des grands propriétaires fonciers, des nobles riches; mais, étant une activité spécialisée et peu honorable, il n'était pas exercé par eux: il était exercé par certains de leurs esclaves ou par des hommes libres à leur service. D'autre part, des citoyens 'pauvres', c'est-à-dire ne possédant pas assez de biens pour ne pas devoir gagner leur vie, exerçaient le commerce maritime pour leur compte, dans l'espoir de s'enrichir rapidement et de pouvoir ainsi abandonner le commerce même et toute autre activité lucrative. Alors que voyager pour commercer était une activité peu honorable, envoyer des agents avec des marchandises faire du commerce convenait parfaitement à la vie noble. Qu'on songe à *Iliade* 7. 467-75, où Euenos, seigneur de Lemnos, envoie des navires chargés de vin (cf. aussi un passage déjà cité de l'*Odyssée* 20. 381-83). Qu'on songe à la célèbre coupe laconienne de la Bibliothèque Nationale de Paris, qui – selon une vieille interprétation qui paraît toujours bonne[26] – représente le roi Arkésilas de Cyrène en train d'assister à la pesée et à l'embarquement de sacs remplis d'une marchandise (laine? silphium?). Qu'on songe enfin aux rêveries de richesse dont parle un poème de Bacchylide cité (ci-dessus). Dans un article qui paraîtra ailleurs,[27] je montre que le nom *Hesiodes* est composé de *hesi*- (*hienai*) et de *odo* (cf. Hésychius, s.v. *oda*) et signifie 'Celui qui envoie des cargaisons de marchandises': le père d'Hésiode, un noble 'pauvre' que la 'pauvreté' avait poussé à faire du commerce, a choisi pour son fils ce nom pour lui souhaiter de pouvoir mener un jour une vie noble.

Si on accepte cette construction hypothétique, on sera amené à attribuer au commerce maritime des fonctions essentielles dans la société grecque archaïque. Pour les nobles riches, qui le faisaient exercer à des gens à leur service, il était l'un des moyens pour acquérir des produits de luxe – source de jouissance, mais aussi de prestige, symboles indispensables de leur *status* social; il était en outre un moyen pour pouvoir disposer, dans les années de disette, d'une quantité de nourriture qui leur permettrait non seulement de maintenir, mais d'élargir leur pouvoir sur les hommes, ainsi que d'augmenter leur richesse. Pour les citoyens 'pauvres', qui l'exerçaient personnellement, il était le moyen de loin le plus efficace pour tenter d'"échapper à la méchantervile pauvreté' (comme le dit Hésiode en parlant de son père) et d'entrer dans le cercle des nobles riches et puissants. Exclu de la vie noble, le commerce maritime était l'une des activités qui la rendaient possible.

Ce que je viens de soutenir n'entraîne pas un retour à la théorie critiquée par J. Hasebroek et, à sa suite, par beaucoup d'autres savants, et d'après laquelle les intérêts commerciaux (recherche de débouchés, compétition pour le contrôle des marchés) auraient été parmi les préoccupations et les motifs principaux de la politique étrangère des cités grecques. Mon hypothèse exclut qu'à l'époque archaïque, il y ait eu un groupe social influent, composé de marchands ou dominé par l'esprit mercantile ('chrématistique'). Selon mon hypothèse, ni les riches qui exerçaient le commerce indirectement, par l'intermédiaire de leurs agents, ni les citoyens 'pauvres' qui l'exerçaient directement pour leur propre compte, n'étaient des marchands. Aux yeux de leurs concitoyens, ils n'étaient pas caractérisés socialement par le fait d'exercer, indirectement ou directement, le commerce. Tout en cherchant le gain, ils gardaient leurs yeux fixés sur les idéaux de la vie noble: luxe, éclat, munificence, prestige, pouvoir politique. Certes, les agents qui exerçaient le commerce pour le compte de citoyens riches, étaient des marchands professionnels; mais ou bien ils n'étaient pas des hommes libres, ou bien, s'ils l'étaient (c'est le cas d'Achillodoros dans la lettre sur plomb de Berezan'), ils ne pouvaient pas – étant au service de tel ou tel citoyen riche – constituer un groupe social compact, capable d'influencer la politique de la cité. Je pense en outre qu'à l'époque archaïque (mais aussi plus tard), la production de marchandises (autrement dit, la production destinée à la vente) occupait, dans l'ensemble de l'économie des sociétés grecques et des sociétés barbares avec lesquelles les Grecs commerçaient, une place trop modeste, et que, d'autre part, elle était géographiquement trop répandue, pour qu'une âpre compétition pour la conquête et le contrôle des marchés fût inévitable. A mon avis, ceux qui avaient des produits à vendre, susceptibles de rencontrer les besoins et les goûts d'acheteurs grecs ou barbares, avaient normalement de très bonnes chances de les vendre avec profit, à un endroit ou à un autre, en contre-partie d'autres produits. Cela, bien entendu, ne saurait être démontré; encore une fois, je ne m'appuie que sur la vraisemblance. Je ne peux pas exclure que des intérêts commerciaux aient parfois contribué à faire croître la rivalité entre telle et telle autre cité.

Pour revenir au sujet qui nous concerne ici directement, on remarquera que si on accepte les considérations que j'ai faites ci-dessus sur les conditions de la production céréalière et sur les groupes sociaux susceptibles d'acheter des céréales, il en ressort que les céréales étaient parmi les marchandises les plus constamment demandées, même si les marchés d'écoulement – comme d'ailleurs, quoique sans doute dans une mesure moins grande, les marchés d'approvisionnement – variaient d'une année à l'autre; et que, si le rôle social du commerce en général était important, celui du commerce des céréales revêtait une importance particulière.

Certes, on hésitera à appeler le commerce des céréales de l'époque archaïque un 'commerce de masse', comme on peut le faire pour celui de l'époque classique. Mais quel qu'ait été son volume, son rôle social était essentiel.

Warsaw   BENEDETTO BRAVO

NOTES

1. Il y vingt ans, une étude très lucide de quelques questions fondamentales relatives au commerce grec archaïque a été faite par Ed. Will dans le cadre de son rapport (intitulé 'La Grèce archaïque') à la Second International Conference of Economic History, Aix-en-Provence (1962) I: *Trade and Politics in the Ancient World* (1965) 41-96, notamment 45-6, 57, 68-71, 76-8, 84. (Voir aussi la discussion qui a suivi le rapport d'Ed. Will, 97-115.) Parmi les recherches plus récentes, voir notamment M. M. Austin, *Greece and Egypt in the archaic age*, PCPS Suppl. 2 (1970), spécialement 8-9, 11-14, 22-45, et notes à 49-52, 58-75; Ch. G. Starr, *The economic and social growth of early Greece, 800-500 B.C.* (1977); A. Mele, *Il commercio greco arcaico. Prexis ed emporie* (1979). Pour une discussion du livre de Mele ainsi que de quelques thèses de celui de Starr, voir mon article 'Commerce maritime et noblesse en Grèce archaïque', à paraître dans *DHA*.

2. Voir notamment T. J. Dunbabin, *The Greeks and their Eastern neighbours* (1957); J. Boardman, *The Greeks overseas, their early colonies and trade* (rev. ed., 1980), 35-84.

3. Dunabin (n.2) 28-30; R. M. Cook, 'Die Bedeutung der bemalten Keramik für den griechischen Handel', *JDAI* 74 (1959) 122; Starr (n. 1) 60-1. Situation analogue en Egypte: voir Austin (n. 1) 8, 37, Boardman (n. 2) 42, 44, 46-7, 53-4 semble penser que, si l'on ne trouve que très peu de céramique greque dans les pays du Levant avant la fin du VIe siècle, c'est qu'il n y avait pas encore de 'commerce organisé' de la céreamique. Cette explication me paraît étrange.

4. On a tiré d'Homère et d'Hésiode des arguments pour prouver qu'au VIIIe siècle et au début du VIIe, l'huile d'olive n'était employée que comme onguent, et qu'une culture spécialisée de l'olivier n'a commencé que plus tard: voir récemment Mele, (n. 1) 75, et O. Murray, *Early Greece* (1980) 46. Ces arguments se ramènent à l'*argumentum e silentio*; or, celui-ci ne me paraît pas, dans ce cas, convaincant. Les poètes épiques n'avaient pas à décrire tous les détails de la cuisine ou de l'éclairage; et Hésiode n'a pas entrepris de décrire en détail tout ce que peut produire une modeste propriété: le produit qui l'intéresse, c'est le blé, et on comprend cela aisément. D'ailleurs, même si l'huile n'était employée que comme onguent (et pour la fabrication de parfums), elle aurait pu faire l'objet d'un commerce. Mele parle en effet d'un commerce aristocratique de l'huile. Murray est d'un autre avis; il écrit: 'It seems that there was no specialized cultivation of the olive: this had to wait for a change in habits of consumption, and the growth of a trade in staple commodities between different areas; for the concentration on olive oil in Attica from the sixth century onwards presupposes both a more than local market and the ability to organize corn imports'. J'essaie, dans le présent article, justement de montrer qu'un marché 'more than local' et un 'trade in staple commodities between different areas' existaient déjà au VIIIe siècle. Remarquons ici en passant que rien ne prouve qu'il y ait eu en Attique, depuis le VIe siècle, une 'concentration' de l'agriculture dans la production de l'huile d'olive: voir *supra* 21-2.

5. Starr (n. 1) 65 (aussi 77).

6. Cf. les considérations de Starr (n. 1) 61-62.

7. Pour le moment, voir mon article 'Remarques sur les assises sociales, les formes d'organisation et la terminologie du commerce maritime grec à l'époque archaïque', *DHA* 3 (1977) 30, 33-40; mais ce que j'ai écrit sera radicalement corrigé et considérablement développé dans un article que je suis en train d'écrire et qui concerne 'une famille de mots méconnue'. Quelques remarques se trouvent aussi dans l'article inédit mentionné ci-dessus, note 1.

8. Voir par exemple T. J. Dunbabin, *The Western Greeks* (1948) 7, 214, 246; G. Vallet, *Rhégion et Zancle* (1958) 207.

9. H. Maehler, dans son édition *Bakchylides, Lieder und Fragmente, griechisch und deutsch* (1968) 152, après avoir rappelé qu'Alexandros fils d'Amyntas a régné depuis 498 jusqu'à 454, écrit: 'Da das Lied eher für einen jungen, lebenslustigen Herrn geschrieben zu sein scheint, wird es schon in den neunziger Jahren entstanden sein'. Mais, à mon avis, rien n'indique que le poème ait été écrit 'für einen jungen, lebenslustigen Herrn'. Si, aux vers 6-9, il est question des désirs érotiques que le vin suscite chez les jeunes gens participant au *sumposion*, c'est que le poème que Bacchylide envoie à Alexandros est destiné à être chanté dans un *sumposion* et entend, au début, évoquer certains traits caractéristiques de tout *sumposion*. Bien sûr, Alexandros participera au *sumposion*; mais les hommes mûrs et les vieillards participaient aux *sumposia* tout aussi bien que les jeunes gens (voir p. ex. Xénophane, fr. 1 Diels-Kranz, vers 17-18). Que ce qui est dit des jeunes gens aux vers 6-9 ne concerne pas nécessairement Alexandros, ressort du fait que ce qui est dit des buveurs rêvant la richesse aux vers 13-16 ne le concerne certainement pas (en effet, lui, il est assez riche pour ne pas rêver des navires chargés de blé).

10. Cf. M. M. Austin et P. Vidal-Naquet, *Economic and social history of ancient Greece. An introduction* (1977) 69; et déjà Austin (n. 1) 35; et sur le commerce entre Grecs et Egyptiens, 35-40, 69-74. Ma liste hypothétique des marchandises qu'on échangeait est un peu plus large que celle que propose Austin.

11. V. V. Lapin, *Grečeskaja kolonizacija Severnogo Pričernomor'ja* (1966) 71-6; Ja. V. Domanskij, 'Zametki o haraktere torgovyh svjazej Grekov s tuzemnym mirom Severnogo Pričernomor'ja v VII v. do n.e.', *Arheologičeskij Sbornik Gosud. Ermitaža*, 12 (1970) 47-53.

12. A. Wąsowicz, *Olbia pontique et son territoire* (1975) 29-31.

13. Lapin (n. 11) 60-183, et spécialement 86-147.

14. Cette conclusion a déjà été tirée explicitement par Mele (n. 1) 102 n. 91, sur la base des données réunies par Wąsowicz (n. 12) 31 sqq. et 50 sqq.

15. Il vaut la peine de signaler que dans l'établissement grec de l'île de Berezan', on a mis au jour, entre autres, un petit trésor du VIe siècle, composé de quelques bijoux d'or (une paire de boucles d'oreille et deux pendentifs) et de quatre monnaies d'or, et contenu dans un petit vase peint du VIe siècle, qui se trouvait dans une couche archéologique de la seconde moitié du VIIe et de la première moitié du VIe siècle: voir la brève communication ('tezisy') de P. O. Karyškovskij et de V. V. Lapin dans les Actes d'un colloque tenu en 1977 à Chaltubo: *Problemy grečeskoj kolonizacii Severnogo i Vostočnogo Pričernomor'ja* (1979) 105. Puisque le recueil où la brève note de Karyškovskij et de Lapin a été publiée risque d'être difficile à trouver en Occident, il me semble utile de rapporter ici les renseignements que ces savants donnent au sujet des quatre monnaies, ainsi que la datation qu'ils en proposent. Il s'agit d'un statère (13,61 grammes), portant à l'avers la représentation d'une tête de félin (d'une lionne?) en profil, et de trois *tritai* (respectivement 4,67 gr.; 4,52 gr.; 4,38 gr.), portant à l'avers une rosette (deux de ces *tritai* ont été exécutées avec une même matrice); le revers de toutes ces monnaies présente 'une enfonçure de configuration complexe ("carré enfoncé")'. Selon les deux savants, 'ces monnaies ont été frappées en Ionie (le plus probablement à Milet, peut-être à Erythrai). Le statère date du dernier tiers du VIIe siècle avant n.è., les *tritai* datent des premières décennies du VIe'. Ces monnaies appartiennent donc 'aux plus anciennes monnaies du monde grec'. 'Le trésor fut enfoui, ainsi qu'on peut le supposer, par l'un des premiers colons, et il constitue un témoignage intéressant aussi bien sur les rapports de l'établissement de Berezan' avec la métropole, que sur le bien-être économique des colons'. – A mon avis, la datation de ces monnaies proposée par Karyškovskij et Lapin est très invraisemblable. Autant que je sache, les numismates, aujourd'hui, pensent généralement que les cités grecques d'Asie Mineure n'ont commencé à frapper des monnaies d'or que dans la seconde moitié du VIe siècle (voir C. M. Kraay, *Archaic and*

classical Greek coins (1976). De toute façon, même si les monnaies en question étaient aussi anciennes que Karyškovskij et Lapin l'ont dit, il ne serait pas légitime de soutenir que ce trésor appartenait à l'un des premiers colons de l'établissement de l'île de Berezan' (rappelons que l'existence de celui-ci est attestée archéologiquement depuis le dernier tiers du VIIe siècle). En effet, il serait parfaitement possible que les monnaies aient été enfouies quelques décennies (voire plusieurs décennies) après la date de leur émission. En outre, si l'on suppose – comme il est raisonnable de le faire et comme Karyškovskij et Lapin l'ont fait – qu'elles ont été enfouies, le contexte archéologique du trésor (deuxième moitié du VIIe – première moitié du VIe siècle) indique que cela a eu lieu après le milieu du VIe siècle: en effet, s'il a été enfoui, le trésor s'est trouvé nécessairement à un niveau inférieur à la surface du sol de l'époque où il a été enfoui. Le vase qui contenait le trésor est datable, selon Karyškovskij et Lapin, du VIe siècle. Il faudra donc conclure que c'est probablement vers la fin du VIe siècle que le trésor a été enfoui.

16. Starr (n. 1) 165, soutient que 'there is no reason to believe that the Greeks even of the cities were fed by any other than native resources until some point in the sixth century – by which time their workshops were producing the wares which could be used to pay for imported grain'. Puis, à p. 176, il soutient que la politique de Pisistrate et des Pisistratides dans les Détroits indique que c'est à partir du milieu du VIe siècle que commence, à Athènes, le besoin de blé importé. Mele (n. 1) 104-7 (aussi 102), situe entre les dernières décennies du VIIe et les premières du VIe siècle le début de l'importation de blé dans les cités grecques; il lie ce phénomène à la croissance d'un *demos* urbain ('ceti medi', 109), et il en voit un indice dans le développement d'une céramique produite en série dans la période entre 620 et 580.

17. Sur l'équilibre instable qui caractérise la production agricole dans le monde grec, autrement dit sur la fréquence des disettes, voir A. Jardé, *Les céréales dans l'antiquité grecque. I: La production* (1925) 144.

18. Cette loi est certainement de Solon, car Plutarque indique le numéro de l'*axon* où elle était inscrite. (Le savant inconnu dont Plutarque dépend, a probablement lu les lois de Solon non pas sur les *axones*, mais sur les *kurbeis*; mais le texte inscrit sur les *kurbeis* contenait des indications sur les numéros des *axones* contenant tel ou tel groupe de lois. Voir R. Stroud, *The axones and kyrbeis of Drakon and Solon* (1979).) Je suppose que les drachmes dont il est question dans cette loi ainsi que dans d'autres lois authentiquement soloniennes, sont des drachmes pré-monétaires.

19. Voir Ph. Gauthier, 'Notes sur l'étranger et l'hospitalité en Grèce et à Rome', *Ancient Society* 4 (1973) 1-21.

20. Will (n. 1) 77.

21. Will (n. 1) 70.

22. R. Meiggs et D. Lewis, *GHI* (1969) 65, résument ainsi ce passage de l'inscription: 'Curses are invoked against [...] those who prevent the import of corn or re-export it when it has been imported'. Cette interprétation est certainement fausse: le verbe *anothein* ne peut pas signifier 're-exporter'; il ne peut signifier que 'repousser'. F. Hiller v. Gaertringen, dans *Sylloge*³ 37-8, avait compris le passage correctement: 'prohibeat, ne inducatur'.

23. Je dis 'ou une partie', parce que je suppose que certains parmi les artisans libres possédaient un peu de terre.

24. Mele (n. 1) 77, est d'un autre avis: 'L'eroe aristocratico [...] evidentemente non importa cereali, ma semmai li vende'. Cela ne me paraît pas du tout évident.

25. Bravo (n. 7) 1-59 – article qui sera partiellement corrigé par l'article inédit mentionné ci-dessus, note 1. Voir aussi 'Une lettre sur plomb de Berezan': colonisation et modes de contact dans le Pont', *DHA* 1 (1974) 123, 149-54, et, pour une meilleure édition et une meilleure interprétation de la 'lettre d'Achillodoros', 'Sulân. Représailles et justice privée contre des étrangers dans les cités grecques', *Annali della Scuola Normale Superiore di Pisa*, s. 3, 10 (1980) 879-85.

26. Pour une interprétation différente, voir F. Chamoux, *Cyrène sous la monarchie des Battiades* (1953) 257-8, et C. M. Stibbe, *Lakonische Vasenmaler des sechsten Jahrhunderts v.Chr.* (1972) Textband, 115-7.

27. 'Le nom Hésiodos: un témoignage sur la société grecque archaïque'.

4. FOREIGN TRADE AND FOREIGN POLICY IN ARCHAIC GREECE

There is growing archaeological evidence that the Mycenaean trade, antecedent to the trade of Archaic Greece, was extensive, with foreign markets in the East, in Sicily, and in Southern Italy.

Foreign trade at this time was palace-based; the import of copper, as we learn from the Linear-B tablets found in Pylos, was a royal monopoly; implicit is a corresponding centralization of the export trade. As for the goods exported, the unearthed pottery suggests only that wine and oil were among them, though there are clues to other exports as well, textiles, for instance. Nor have we any good evidence as to what proportion of the 'imports' entered the country in the form of gifts, of an organized exchange of goods, what in the form of booty, and what as the result of 'royal' or private piracy on the high seas.

With the disintegration of the Mycenaean Monarchies, there came the disintegration of this entire early system of trade. It was not until the middle of the 9th century that the first foreign-made luxury articles appeared in Greece, primarily in Attica; as for Greek exports, the first ceramics of Hellenic origin found in the East are those in al-Mina from the last decade of the century.

As far as we can tell from the poor archaeological evidence and from epic tradition, the long-distance trade that again evolved now in the Protogeometric Period combined traditions of the Mycenaean practices with Phoenician, especially Sidonian, trade initiative.

The 'glorious Phoenicians' (*phoinikes agauoi*) naturally traded with the *basileis*, or the *prekteres* they had commissioned. The 'famous' Sidonian sailors were joint owners of the trading ships they sailed in; they acted jointly, but independently of the domestic authorities. They offered everything from exquisite silver goblets (*Iliad* 23. 740) to cheap trinkets (*Odyssey* 14. 287) for sale, winning the good will of the *basileis* with gifts. Their complementary activities included the transport of passengers (not only merchants! *Odyssey* 13. 271), and on occasion, kidnapping and slave-trading (cf. the story of Eumaios). The picture of Phoenician-Greek trade Homer presents is one of *private* traders doing business with *basileis*, offering them mainly luxury articles. That is the Sidonians, who initiated this trade. They sought out the Achaean markets, presented their wares, and chose the exchange articles. Small as the volume of this trade was, it had enormous significance in opening trade routes that were subsequently to be used in the trade of staples.

The *basileis* traded among themselves, too; they traded 'gifts' in the knowledge or hope of reciprocal favours. As yet, these exchanges served the mutual satisfaction of current needs; there was no element of profit, of *kerdos* in them. Euneos of

Lemnos, son of Jason, sold 1,000 measures of wine to the two Atreides; in return, he received copper, iron, leather, livestock and slaves (*Iliad* 7. 467). Mentes, King of the Taphii, traded iron for copper (*Odyssey* 1. 184).

The author of the *Odyssey* thus distinguished the regular trade for profit carried on by the Phoenicians from the occasional exchanges to satisfy momentary needs practiced by the Achaeans, and held the former to be a condition of civilized existence (Cf. *Odyssey* 9. 125).

The picture we get from Hesiod in part confirms, in part modifies that of the Homeric epics. In Hesiod's world, trade is a supplementary form of income for well-off farmers, those who regularly have surplus produce to sell. It is for this, and not only for meteorologic reasons, that he suggests the 50 days following the summer equinox (from about June 21 to Aug. 10) as the best days for seaborne trade. The winds then are favourable; the harvest is over, and the grapes not yet ripe. The trade Hesiod tells about is in some sense more primitive than that we find in Homer as it describes contemporary practice, rather than some idealized past; in other respects, however, it is more sophisticated. It is more primitive in that it is a trade with neighbouring parts, in the region between Asia Minor and Boiotia; landowners are trading, rather than professional traders, with their own surplus produce. But it is more sophisticated in that at least on one side it is the trade of raw materials, large quantities of grain, 'the gift of the earth' (*Works and Days* 31. 689), the trade is carried on in 'big ships' (smaller ones are used only to minimize the risks) requiring a considerable number of sailors (*hetairoi, dmoes, thetes*). In exchange, the traders get some luxury articles: wine from Byblos (589), but also slaves and livestock (308, 406). It is an established trade route, with stable markets. Hesiod often warns his audience against taking risks, but he is talking only about the risks at sea, not the commercial ones. Hesiod's Greece was already geared to importing grain from overseas; the demand, it seems, was greater than the supply.

Hesiod's account agrees with Homer's, however, in that the traders were not peripheral social elements, but well-off landowners with yields well above what was necessary to satisfy their own needs, men with ships and sailors of their own. The *polis* as such took no part in trade; but the traders belonged to the *polis* establishment. A number of other sources confirm this: of the few traders of Archaic Greece known to us by name, Charaxos of Lesbos, Sappho's brother, Sostratos of Aigina, Phobos of Phokaia ἔχων δύναμιν καὶ βασιλικὸν ἀξίωμα παρέπλευσεν εἰς Πάριον ἰδίων ἕνεκα πραγμάτων (FGrHist 262 F 7). And others, too, mostly belonged to the aristocracy of their cities even before making their fortune as traders. Plutarch (*Solon* 2. 7) finds nothing amiss in Solon's being a trader, and marshals a host of examples to support his point.

The above picture of early Greek trade c. 700 is complemented, confirmed and somewhat modified by archaeological finds. The letter of complaint written on a lead tablet and found in Berezany in the Ukraine was sent by an agent of an aristocratic landowner-trader of Miletos, whose trade contacts, it seems, extended quite a bit further than Hesiod would have imagined. By this time, the first *emporia* had come into being (al-Mina, Tell Sukas, Tell el-Basit, and in the West, Pithekusai), and some colonies had been founded, especially in the western parts.

The *emporia*, naturally, were founded with trade in mind, and the *poleis* which had had a hand in organizing and financing them must have had definite economic expectations to take such risks. Thus, small though they were and little as we know about them, the very fact of the *emporia*'s existence argues for the significance of overseas trade at that time. This summary conclusion calls for some complementary comments.

Although researchers have emphasized the agrarian character of most of the colonies, the *apoikiai*, many of these not specifically commercial settlements were centers of trade as well. Among them were the following: (*a*) all those colonies which were naturally unsuited for agriculture: e.g. Zankle, Rhegion, Zagora on the island of Andros, (*b*) most of those founded with the support of the local population or their representatives; they would never have given such support had they not expected it to serve the economic interests of the local population. Such settlements were Naukratis *par excellence*, Abydos (Strabo 13 C 590), Massilia, Megara Hyblaia, and the Hispanic colonies, Emporion (= Ampurias), Mainake, and so on.

The establishment and sustained existence of all these settlements prove the voluminousness and profitability of overseas trade.

Another indication of the volume of trade involved is the efforts that were made to introduce bigger, faster and safer ships. In Hesiod already we read of traders loading their goods on big ships where every inch of space could be put to use. Corinth and Phokaia introduced new ships, the former the *strongyle*; while the latter adapted the *triremes* for purposes of trade. Further evidence is the building of the *diolkos* across the Isthmus, something that would hardly have been undertaken without the certainty of frequent use; as well as the construction at this time of piers and other docking facilities in a number of *poleis*. All this is sufficient to prove three points: the great volume of archaic overseas trade; the fact that a great part of goods transported consisted of staples; that the leaders of the poleis involved in trade had an interest in maintaining it. Of course, when we speak of the 'great volume' of this trade we can mean, for lack of statistics, only that it was great enough and vital enough for settlements to be established at certain junctions in the trade routes, for innovations in shipping to be introduced, and for the *poleis* to be committed to ensuring its continuation. For trade at that time could bring wealth not only to those directly involved in it, but to entire cities: Spina at the mouth of the Po grew rich on overseas trade (Dion. Hal. 1.18.4), as did Syracuse, if we are to believe the tyrant Gelon. The aristocracy, of course, profited from this indirectly. The Bacchiadai of Corinth 'enjoyed the fruits of trade without a care' (Strabon).

Given the modest size, population and productivity of the *poleis*, then, we can speak of a *relatively* 'significant' trade in Archaic Greece, a trade which, from the beginning concentrated on staples. Primary among these probably were the metals:

iron ore, and much smaller quantities of non-ferrous metals. When al-Mina was excavated, it was already supposed that the Euboian and then Corinthian traders working in the area got here the iron ore and iron objects originating in the mines of Urartu in the Caucasus. Pithekusai (Ischia) in the north specialized primarily in mediating the products of its hinterland and Etruria, both exceedingly rich in iron ore. True enough, the Euboian traders from Chalkis and Eretria working here initially could easily find iron ore closer to home, for instance in Euboia, on the islands of the Aegean, and on the Peloponnesus; in the early Archaic Period, however, when hoplite warfare and the use of iron arms became general, the demand for iron ore must have been insatiable, and the deposits of central and southern Italy so accessible as to permit practically surface mining. The non-ferrous metals came primarily from farther west, from Transalpine Gaul and Hispania, and in the case of tin from Cornwall.

The most important staple next to metals was grain. Hesiod already tells us of traders transporting 'Demeter's gifts' in big ships headed for areas poor in grains, probably from Boiotia and Euboia to the Greek poleis of Asia Minor. Hellas, at that time, was still an exporter of grain. The turning-point from a period of plenty to one of scarcity in grains was sometime about the end of the 7th century, under circumstances difficult to reconstruct fully, but which were behind changes such as Solon's reforms in Athens, mass colonization or the switch to tyranny elsewhere. The very fact that most of the colonies were established in areas suited for agriculture shows that the *poleis* founding them had neither land nor food enough. The curse pronounced at the beginning of the 5th century by the Island of Teos on any trader exporting grain, a curse that was to follow his whole family, shows what passions the scarcity of grains had aroused. Nor is there any evidence for thinking it reflects a temporary crisis in grain supplies.

In the 6th century, the outlines of the major grain routes of the future could already be seen: from the rich agrarian regions of Sicily and Southern Italy to Corinth, and from there on to the other Peloponnesian cities, with the *diolkos* linking the two harbours facilitating the distribution of the food staples. The other great centre was the Pontus region, in the western half of which, as Herodotus tells us, 'grain is sown not only for consumption, but also for sale' (Hdt. 4.1). In the East, it was the towns of the Propontis, for instance Byzantion, which probably mediated the trade directed toward Miletos, the major entrepôt in the east to the end of the 6th century, when, as is commonly known (Hdt. 7.147) Aigina took over this role; it was grain ships headed for Aigina that Xerxes could have captured. By this time, around 480 B.C., the shortage of grain in most of Hellas had become permanent and generally known. Bacchylides knew and rated highly the fact that the King of Macedon had got rich on his grain trade with Egypt (Frg. 20 B Snell): χρυσῷ δ᾽ἐλέφαντι τε μαρμαίρουσιν οἶκοι/πυροφόροι δὲ κατ᾽ αἰγλάεντα πόντον/νᾶες ἄγουσιν ἀπ᾽ Αἰγύπτου μέγιστον/πλοῦτον ... and he considers it a permanent source of income. Gelon, tyrant of Syracuse at about the same time,

confidently promises to ship to Hellas sufficient grain for the duration of the
Persian Wars (Hdts. 7. 158). Herodotus also tells us that Greek merchants went to
Egypt 'as was their custom' even during the Persian Wars in search of grain (Hdts.
3. 139). Naukratis was built on the availability of Egyptian grain, and had been a
centre of grain trade even before a number of poleis joined to develop it as an
entrepôt c. 560. In quite another direction, about 2 km. from Olbia on the Black
Sea, Greek vase fragments dating back to the 6th century have been found, left
probably in exchange for grain.

To sum up: the considerable grain trade of the early 5th century, which, by 451
B.C. became a political issue of such weight in Athens that it led to new restrictions
on Athenian citizenship, and was to become, in the 4th century, the central issue of
Athenian politics, had roots which can be traced back to the Archaic Period, at
least to the beginning of the 6th century.

Other imports of significance besides metals and grains were the marble and
other stones necessary in building, and the hardwood needed for ship-building.
These, unlike the metals and grain that came from the 'barbarian' areas, came from
regions on the periphery of the Greek world.

The degree to which the various Greek *poleis* were interested in the foreign trade
in staples was by no means uniform, and was liable to change with the passing of
time. Various circumstances determined the stands they took on the matter of
foreign trade, and we should beware of thinking of any of these stands as
representative. Aigina appears to have been at one end of the scale; totally lacking
in natural resources, it played a vital role in the trade and redistribution of staples.
Here, the interests of rich traders (e.g. Sostratos) coincided with the interests of the
polis as a whole. Aigina's pressing need for Egyptian grain motivated her active part
in the founding of Naukratis; the need to secure the route to it led to the
establishment of Kydonia; the need to keep the upper hand set her consistently
against Samos; the need to secure the means wherewith to pay for the imports made
her take the silver mines of Siphnos from the Samians (Hdts. 3. 57); the need to
protect the vital interests of her potters who had to rely on import clay and thus
worked with a bigger overhead made Aigina take the unprecedented step of barring
Athenian pottery from her territory (Hdts. 5. 88); the need to minimize her
dependence on Egypt made her turn also to Pontus for grain; and the need to
protect her economic interests in the 'east' explain her *medismos*. Thus, although
the sources make no explicit references to *vital* economic interests, the policies
adopted appear so far consistent with known economic interests that one could
hardly doubt their being economically motivated. And though Aigina might
appear an extreme case in this regard, she is hardly likely to have been unique.

Somewhat different was the situation of highly urbanized *poleis*, like Chalkis,
Eretria, later Corinth, most of the Ionian cities, and Athens from the 6th century
on, which also had a vital interest in the import of raw materials but, unlike Aigina,
had agricultural products and handicrafts to trade for them. These enjoyed what

was tantamount to a monopoly of the trade in these products in the *apoikiai* they had founded. The *apoikiai*, obviously, were not established for the purpose of such trade; but the kinship, religious and political ties they had with the founding *poleis* made them dependable suppliers of staples. The advantages of the trade monopolies these 'colonial' relatives permitted were nothing new; Miletos had enjoyed them in its Pontus colonies, Phokaia in Massilia, the Euboian cities in al-Mina in the east and Pithekusai in the west, Corinth in Magna Graecia and partly in Sicily, and, before Lycurgus' reform, Sparta in Tarentum.

These same *poleis* carried on trade also in areas where they enjoyed no 'colonial' advantages (e.g. Corinth in Etruria). Here, their individual craftsmen and tradesmen had to rely on the quality of the product they offered and on personal ties for business success. The pottery unearthed is our only empirical evidence for this aspect of archaic trade: some of the most beautiful Athenian vases have been found in Sicily and Southern Italy. We might risk the generalization that the colonial trade monopolies concentrated on the import of staples; while trade was 'individual' where so-called 'luxury' items changed hands. We must note, however, that the *poleis* refrained from using *sui generis* economic means to further their interests in both types of trade, being satisfied to guarantee the safety of the trade routes and of the merchants engaged in trade. In this, the interests of all the *poleis* coincided, and the attempts to monopolize any given market were overruled by the need to cooperate.

That all this was so had a great deal to do with the fact that the Greeks' trading partners were, in the long run, the 'barbarians' – the Scythians, the Egyptians, the Etruscans, and the indigenous population of Sicily and Magna Graecia. The peculiarity of this trade was that it was only the Greeks who were in it for staples; their partners got mostly luxury articles in exchange. The Greeks' disadvantage in respect of raw materials was compensated for by their use of coins, by their more developed technology, the artistry and formal variety of their export goods, their higher level of economic organization and of political consciousness. It is this latter fact that accounts for the mutual respect generally shown for the other *poleis'* sphere of interest, for the lack of genuine competition, for the willingness to cooperate with one's rivals. The fragile advantage the Greek *poleis* enjoyed over their barbarian trading partners could not have sustained the shock of out and out economic competition.

It was only occasionally that cooperation among the *poleis* took the organized, legal form it did in the founding and maintenance of Naukratis, wherein 12 cities cooperated, all trying to get the most for themselves, but conscious of their common interests as well. For the most part, cooperation asserted itself only in the practice. Perhaps we could see the effect of such a 'practical' cooperation in the process through which Athenian pottery (black-figured, and then red-figured vases) gradually forced the Corinthian products off the western markets. Starting to proliferate in the first quarter of the 6th century, Athenian vases came to dominate the whole of the Mediterranean, gradually suffering a setback after 450, and losing all their markets by the end of the Peloponnesian Wars.

What is most interesting in all this is that these western regions were not an Athenian sphere of political or military influence at the time of this rapid expansion of trade, nor was any need to establish this felt in the century following (c. 570 on).

Furthermore, although Athens was expanding and Corinth was being pushed economically into the background, no political conflicts resulted: Athens under Peisistratos was an ally of Corinth, and later it was the Corinthians who helped prevent Hippias' forceful return to power (Hdts. 5. 92). The sale of Athenian vases in Southern Italy and Etruria was a matter of individual trade. It failed to become a political issue possibly because the vases went west in Corinthian ships (or perhaps Corcyrean or Ionian) in a spontaneous cooperative venture which thus did not infringe on Corinth's 'colonial' interests.

Such cooperative ventures among the *poleis* were likely to have taken a variety of forms: specialization in certain products, pottery in Athens, fine woollens in Miletos, rough textile staples in Megara, etc.; the uncontested 'monopoly' of certain trade routes by some poleis (e.g. Phokaia's domination of the far western trade). At this phase of expansion *cooperation* seems to have been stronger than *confrontation* in foreign trade.

All this led to a considerable depoliticization of foreign trade in the Greek spheres of interest. Throughout the Mediterranean and along the Pontus there came into being a situation which a researcher of Greek trade in Transalpine Gaul and Hispania has described as 'une association amicale de produits indigènes, grecs et puniques'. For it seems that right to the end of the 6th century the luxury goods available for sale balanced on the whole the staples that needed to be imported.

In the 5th century, after the repulse of the Persians, we find a new surge of urbanization tilting the population balance away from the agricultural producers toward a predominance of consumers (e.g. artisans). It was at that time that the shortage of food in Greece became pressing and permanent. By the 4th century the need for food imports had become a dominating feature of Greek, and particularly Athenian, politics, a matter of keen competition among the *poleis* interested in foreign trade. This, however, is another period altogether.

Budapest   ISTVÁN HAHN

5. LE COMMERCE DES AMPHORES GRECQUES

A la différence de la plupart des autres documents archéologiques qui peuvent contribuer à l'étude des relations commerciales dans le monde grec aux époques classique et hellénistique, les amphores nous offrent le reflet *direct* de transactions portant sur des biens de grande consommation (vin surtout et huile, ainsi que d'autres denrées telles qu'olives et salaisons[1]): comme elles ne valaient pas tant par elles-mêmes que par leur contenu et que leur fabrication ne devait généralement pas poser de problème, elles avaient en effet peu de chances d'être transportées vides sur de longues distances à partir de leur lieu d'origine.[2] Tout un réseau d'échanges peut ainsi se reconstituer, souvent original par rapport à ceux que dessinent la diffusion de la céramique fine ou la circulation monétaire.

Or il se trouve que grâce aux efforts patients d'une poignée de spécialistes, dont la plupart ont travaillé sous l'influence soit du Soviétique B. N. Grakov,[3] soit de l'Américaine V. Grace,[4] nous avons beaucoup progressé au cours du dernier demi-siècle dans la connaissance de ce matériel, et notamment des timbres qui lui étaient parfois apposés avant cuisson: mais sans que l'on ait toujours réussi à assurer le recensement complet de trouvailles surabondantes et une large diffusion à la masse d'informations accumulées dans les fichiers.[5]

Aussi bien les historiens de l'économie antique, séduits par une documentation qui se prêtait bien à des études chiffrées, n'ont-ils pas toujours été à même d'en faire un usage judicieux. C'est pourquoi il me paraît opportun de réfléchir ici aux précautions qu'exige ce type d'informations, ainsi qu'à la portée des conclusions que l'on peut en tirer. Avec l'espoir de répondre à deux exigences très actuelles de l'histoire ancienne: celle de réduire le fossé qui tend à se creuser entre la réflexion historique et la spécialisation érudite et celle de viser à des interprétations plus solides et plus raffinées des données archéologiques[6] – exigences qui, en la matière, sont d'autant plus vivement ressenties en Occident qu'on continue souvent à y vivre dans une tranquille ignorance des efforts accomplis en ce sens par les savants de langue slave.[7]

Des catalogues de timbres établis par les spécialistes pour tel ou tel site les historiens n'ont parfois retenu que le total des exemplaires provenant de tel ou tel centre de production: qu'ils traduisent hâtivement en termes économiques en excipant de textes qui n'en peuvent mais, ou d'arguments de pure vraisemblance aisément réversibles.

Dénonçant ce 'mauvais usage' du matériel amphorique, J.-Y. Empereur[8] a naguère justement critiqué diverses interprétations des données alexandrines et déliennes avancées par M. Rostovtzeff, P. M. Fraser ou Cl. Nicolet. Comment en effet spéculer sur l'importance relative des importations de Thasos, de Rhodes, de Cnide et de l'Occident latin sans tenir compte de la datation de séries qui ne se recouvrent que partiellement, ou pas du tout? Sans tenir compte non plus de la déformation des faits suscitée par la limitation des recherches archéologiques à tel ou tel secteur, à telles ou telles couches de l'occupation humaine (aux dernières années, par exemple, de la Dèlos hellénistique où l'emportent naturellement les timbres cnidiens et latins)? Sans tenir compte enfin, pour chaque centre producteur, du pourcentage de timbres par rapport aux amphores qui, seules, permettent de se faire une idée juste du volume des échanges?

La complexité particulière de cette dernière question exige qu'on s'y attarde. On ne peut en effet y répondre clairement que pour les amphores rhodiennes des IIIe-Ier siècles, qui étaient presque toutes estampillées et chacune sur ses deux anses: ce qui permet d'obtenir aisément une évaluation, approchée par défaut, du nombre des amphores concernées (en divisant par deux le nombre des timbres). Mais le problème est plus difficile à résoudre pour les autres séries – qu'elles portent deux ou, plus généralement, une seule estampille (la règle ayant de surcroît pu varier au cours des âges, comme à Thasos dont les amphores en reçurent au tout début souvent deux, puis une). Car la pratique du timbrage y était plus ou moins répandue, sans que nous disposions pour le moment de beaucoup d'informations précises à ce sujet. A Sinope et Héraclée du Pont, elle s'observerait sur le cinquième ou le sixième des amphores; dans la Thasos de la seconde moitié du IVe et du début du IIIe siècle, elle concerne 80% d'entre elles dans le dépotoir urbain de la porte de Zeus, mais seulement 50% dans l'atelier de Koukos et un peu moins de 47% dans celui de Kalonero;[9] à Kos il est avéré qu'il ne s'agissait que d'une toute petite minorité: si bien que les quelques 1480 timbres de Kos retrouvés à Alexandrie pourraient bien attester des importations au moins égales à celles dont témoignent 80 000 estampilles rhodiennes![10] Mais il subsiste bon nombre de cas encore plus incertains. Comment y remédier? C'est évidemment par le comptage systématique des amphores non-timbrées allant de pair avec telle ou telle série de timbres – d'une part sur les lieux de consommation indigènes ou étrangers et d'autre part dans les dépotoirs des ateliers de production – que l'on pourra peu à peu se doter de coefficients correcteurs. Ceux-ci varieront certainement d'après la série envisagée, probablement aussi à l'intérieur de celle-ci d'après l'époque, mais beaucoup moins sans doute qu'on ne le pense généralement d'après le lieu de trouvailles (puisqu'il semble bien que les amphores exportées n'étaient pas plus fréquemment timbrées que celles qui s'utilisaient dans le territoire même de la cité productrice.[11]

En m'inspirant de travaux soviétiques qui ont de longue date soulevé ce genre de problèmes, j'ajouterai que les historiens se doivent encore d'introduire dans leurs calculs un coefficient supplémentaire, qui tient compte de la capacité (moyenne) des diverses séries d'amphores: celle-ci peut en effet varier du simple au décuple – disons de 4 à une quarantaine de litres! Sans parler du fait que des anses qui se cassent plus facilement que d'autres (celles de Sinope par exemple par rapport à celles de

Rhodes) s'en trouveront surreprésentées dans les catalogues...

Abstraction faite des incertitudes qui continuent à peser sur l'identification et la datation des amphores grecques et de leurs timbres, un long chemin reste donc à parcourir avant que l'on soit en mesure d'en tirer des indications chiffrées, à la fois sérieuses et précises, sur l'importance relative et absolue de tel et tel courant commercial.

Sans vouloir jeter le discrédit sur ces recherches quantitatives, je voudrais néanmoins souligner (ou plutôt signaler, tant cet aspect des choses me paraît méconnu) que le même matériel peut se prêter à une approche différente, qualitative, des échanges commerciaux.

J'en veux pour exemple le livre récent de I. B. Brashinsky sur *Les importations grecques sur le Don inférieur du Ve au IIIe siècle avant notre ère* (Léningrad, 1980), où sont publiées les trouvailles céramiques d'Elisavetovskoe.[12] L'abondance en cet endroit des amphores – d'origine essentiellement héracléote, thasienne et sinopienne – contraste avec la précarité apparente de l'établissement ainsi qu'avec leur diffusion restreinte dans l'arrière-pays (sauf, dans une certaine mesure, le long des fleuves): ce qu'on s'explique au mieux en supposant qu'une grande partie de celles qui étaient importées dans cet *emporion* y étaient mises au rebut après avoir été transvasées dans des récipients souples (outres de peaux) que l'on acheminait par voie de terre vers les zones steppo-forestières du Don moyen ou de la basse Volga (comme on le faisait en Roumanie à Cetaṭeni, Poiana, Coslogeni ou Pietroiu, c'est-à-dire à l'extrémité du réseau danubien et au point de départ des routes transcarpathiques).[13] En cette région où les importations grecques étaient jusque-là très peu nombreuses, Elisavetovskoe joua donc, surtout au IVe et au début du IIIe siècles, un rôle d'intermédiaire et devint un important centre d'échanges (qui échappaient presque totalement à l'économie monétaire puisqu'on n'a trouvé sur place que dix monnaies!).

Les préférences des consommateurs semblent parfois transparaître: du fait que, tout comme à Kaminsky sur le Dniepr, les amphores de Chersonèse Taurique sont relativement nombreuses à Elisavetovskoe, plus nombreuses en tout cas que dans les cités grecques du voisinage, n'est-il pas en effet tentant de conclure que ce vin était particulièrement apprécié des Scythes? Dans d'autres régions, elles-mêmes productrices de vin et d'huile, il serait sans doute possible de déceler si les crus étrangers et locaux avaient la même clientèle.

En situant les importations amphoriques dans l'ensemble des données archéologiques, on peut donc entrevoir les besoins économiques, sociaux et culturels, qu'elles étaient destinées à satisfaire.

Prises en elles-mêmes, elles peuvent également, pour peu qu'elles soient pourvues de timbres, nous renseigner sur l'organisation du commerce d'importation dont elles faisaient l'objet. C'est ainsi que I. B. Brashinsky, notant la surreprésentation de certains éponymes héracléotes, thasiens ou sinopiens à Elisavetovskoe et par conséquent l'inégale répartition dans le temps des cargaisons reçues, l'explique par le caractère 'pulsatile', en cette zone-frontière, des opérations commerciales menées par des sortes de marchands-aventuriers: ce qui se justifie à condition qu'on soit bien sûr d'avoir affaire à un matériel significatif, où la fréquence de certains éponymes ne tient pas, tout simplement, à la concentration des trouvailles... De la surreprésentation, également observable, de certains 'fabricants' l'auteur conclut d'autre part à l'existence de relations directes avec les centres producteurs, excluant l'intervention de redistributeurs installés par exemple dans le détroit du Bosphore Cimmérien. En passant en revue les timbres thasiens de type anciens découverts sur la côte occidentale de la mer Noire, qui se révèlent souvent identiques d'Apollonia à Istria, j'ai moi-même souvent eu l'impression de suivre à la trace des caboteurs thasiens chargés d'amphores provenant de deux ou trois ateliers, de même que l'on devine souvent à partir de quel port s'est faite leur redistribution dans l'arrière-pays: que les produits thasiens du IVe siècle gagnaient les territoires gètes à partir d'Istria, tandis que ceux d'Héraclée empruntaient plutôt la voie de terre venant de Tomis et surtout de Callatis, colonie héracléote.[14] Mais de telles enquêtes ne seront vraiment probantes que le jour où, à défaut de gisements sous-marins, on disposera partout de publications satisfaisantes.

Surtout quand elles sont découvertes en petit nombre dans un site reculé, des amphores d'importation n'impliquent cependant pas toujours des transactions portant sur leur contenu original: car il peut tout aussi bien s'agir de récipients de remploi acheminés, à des fins différentes, d'un grand centre importateur (vraisemblablement voisin). C'est ainsi qu'en Egypte, écrit Hérodote (3. 6-7), 'sont importés de toute la Grèce, et aussi de la Phénicie, d'un bout à l'autre de l'année, des vases pleins de vin; et il est autant dire impossible d'y voir, vide, un seul vase ayant contenu du vin. Où donc, pourrait-on demander, ces vases sont-ils utilisés? C'est ce que je vais dire. Chaque dèmarque a le devoir de rassembler tous les vases qui sont dans sa ville et de les conduire à Memphis; les gens de Memphis doivent les remplir d'eau et les transporter dans ces lieux arides de Syrie dont j'ai parlé. Ainsi, à mesure que des vases arrivent et sont vidés en Egypte, on les transporte en Syrie, où ils rejoignent les anciens. Ce sont les Perses qui ont aménagé de la sorte cette voie d'accès en Egypte en la fournissant d'eau comme il vient d'être dit'. En Egypte ou dans la Dèlos hellénistiques, de semblables remplois sont également bien attestés. V. Grace a donc bien raison d'en inférer que les 38 anses timbrées découvertes à Nessana en Palestine 'must necessarily form a relatively scanty and ambiguous commercial record'[15] ou J. H. Kent de ne pas croire, au vu d'une quinzaine d'anses, que dans les vignobles de Rhénée on consommait beaucoup de vin cnidien et rhodien.[16]

Il me paraît enfin possible de pousser encore un peu plus loin l'exploitation du matériel amphorique, jusque sur le plan idéologique: c'est-à-dire de s'en servir pour préciser l'esprit dans lequel se conduisaient les transactions dont il était l'objet. C'est du moins ce qui ressort des progrès naguère accomplis dans la connaissance des timbres thasiens[17] grâce à la fouille de quelques dépotoirs d'ateliers (Koukos,

Vamvouri Ammoudia, Kalonero).

A partir du moment où il est apparu, sans contestation possible,[18] que dans l'abondante série des timbres dits 'récents' (de 340 environ au milieu de l'époque hellénistique) le seul nom mentionné est celui, non pas d'un marchand de vin ou d'un 'fabricant', mais d'un magistrat annuel, et que le fabricant n'y est représenté que par un emblème renouvelé chaque année, il s'ensuit en effet que la pratique du timbrage à Thasos n'avait aucune finalité publicitaire en faveur de telle ou telle entreprise privée, artisanale ou commerciale.

Du fait que les timbres, surtout à l'époque ancienne, étaient parfois très faiblement imprimés et que les amphores, notamment à Kalonero, étaient recouvertes après cuisson d'un engobe crêmeux qui s'est parfois accumulé dans la cavité du timbre au point de rendre celui-ci illisible et presque indiscernable, j'en déduis même que les consommateurs n'en tenaient aucun compte dans leur choix et n'y cherchaient pas davantage une indication de date. Telle est également la réflexion que suggère à I. B. Brashinsky l'apposition sur des pieds d'amphore (en un endroit par conséquent peu visible) de quelques timbres de magistrats héracléotes.[19]

Je ne crois pas davantage que l'objectif du timbrage ait été d'identifier le récipient (et encore moins son contenu) comme thasien aux yeux des consommateurs étrangers: parce qu'il semble bien, que l'on retrouve à l'extérieur un pourcentage d'amphores non-timbrées sensiblement égal à celui qui existe dans l'île même de Thasos; parce qu'il arrivait aussi, à Thasos comme ailleurs, que l'on timbrât les tuiles qui n'étaient que rarement exportées; parce qu'enfin tous les timbres thasiens étaient loin de comporter un ethnique ou des armes parlantes. C'est donc que la forme même de l'amphore suffisait à en dénoncer l'origine (si tant est que le consommateur s'en souciât). Il en allait des timbres amphoriques comme des monnaies: la mention (éventuelle) de l'ethnique avait moins pour but de les identifier que de les authentifier.[20]

Il en ressort que le consommateur devait être parfaitement indifférent à l'existence ou non d'un timbre sur l'amphore. On pourrait s'expliquer ainsi, et non par la maladresse ou l'ignorance des graveurs, la présence de timbres anépigraphes sur certaines imitations thraco-gètes d'amphores rhodiennes.[21] Corrélativement, on ne saurait postuler qu'un timbre non explicite, un monogramme par exemple, doit être d'origine locale sous prétexte qu'"un bollo di questo tipo puo avere un significato soltanto in una zona limitata dov'è noto il senso dell'abbreviatura'.[22] Voilà qui, sans nous faire verser dans le primitivisme, suggère une psychologie de consommateur sensiblement différente de celle que nous connaissons et nous met en garde contre l'anachronisme si facile à commettre en la matière.

Il ne me paraît donc pas douteux que le timbrage des amphores (et des tuiles) procédait d'un contrôle administratif. Mais qui ne concernait pas leur commercialisation à l'étranger: ne serait-ce, outre les raisons déjà avancées, que parce que nombre de cités exportatrices de vins réputés ignoraient cette pratique. C'était plutôt, peut-on supposer, un contrôle s'exerçant au stade de la fabrication.

Mais cela ne nous dit toujours pas exactement pourquoi on a timbré à une certaine époque les amphores, ou plus précisément pourquoi dans un même atelier (comme il ressort des dépotoirs thasiens de Koukos, Vamvouri Ammoudia et Kalonero) certaines amphores étaient timbrées et d'autres pas, dans des proportions telles que le timbrage ne saurait avoir porté sur de simples échantillons. L'hypothèse généralement admise (celle, entre autres, de V. Grace), selon laquelle il s'agirait d'une garantie de capacité, ne me satisfait en effet pas: parce que je doute de la possibilité du potier d'affirmer avant cuisson la *stricte* conformité de son produit à un modèle donné (si cette conformité n'est pas stricte, on n'en voit pas l'utilité); parce que, de fait, les mesures opérées sur des amphores timbrées (généralement autres que thasiennes) ne sont guère convaincantes;[23] parce que je ne conçois pas l'intérêt de produire des récipients (et *a fortiori* des tuiles...) dont les mesures étaient proclamées, par l'absence de timbres, non garanties; et aussi parce que cette hypothèse me semble par trop relever d'un souci de *fair trade*. Au moins à titre provisoire, je préfère donc laisser la question pendante (dans l'attente, notamment, des mesures qui seront faites sur d'importantes séries d'amphores, timbrées ou non, naguère découvertes à Thasos). Nous connaissons si peu du contrôle économique exercé par les magistrats des cités grecques que bien d'autres solutions sont envisageables, en particulier dans une perspective fiscale.

Ces prolégomènes à une étude du commerce des amphores grecques passeront peut-être pour trop critiques, voire pessimistes. Certaines illusions, d'inspiration économiste ou historiciste, y sont en effet dénoncées; mais de nouvelles voies de recherche y sont également indiquées.

Celles-ci ne sont pas sans implications idéologiques et exigent parallèlement, pour être pleinement fructueuses, une autre pratique de terrain: que le matériel amphorique cesse d'être considéré comme un simple sous-produit des activités archéologiques et impose aussi parfois aux fouilleurs une stratégie originale, orientée vers la solution de problèmes spécifiques. Le principal obstacle au progrès des connaissances tient largement, en ce secteur de la recherche, à des habitudes de pensée et à des traditions institutionnelles qu'il n'est certes pas facile de renverser.

Rennes   YVON GARLAN

NOTES

1. Le contenu des amphores découvertes au cours de fouilles terrestres ou maritimes est le plus souvent difficile à déterminer. En certains cas, cependant, on a noté que leur paroi était enduite de résine, comme dans l'épave de Kyrénia: H. W. Swing et M. L. Katzev, 'The Kyrenia shipwreck: a fourth-century B.C. Greek merchant ship', dans *Marine archaeology*, ed. D. J. Blackman (1973) 341. Pour ce qui est de l'huile, on a songé à analyser les microéléments qu'elle a pu laisser dans les parois poreuses (J.

Condamin, F. Formenti, M. O. Metais, M. Michel et P. Blond, 'The application of gas chromatography to the tracing of oil in ancient amphorae', *Archaeometry* 18 (1976) 195-201). Mais il faut bien avouer que c'est généralement à coup d'arguments de vraisemblance (réputation de l'huile et du vin locaux) que nous décidons de la destination de tel ou tel type d'amphores. La grande variété des denrées ainsi transportées est bien attestée: mais j'ai quelque mal à croire qu'elle s'étendait à des produits relativement légers comme les noix d'Héraclée du Pont (Yu. G. Vinogradov et N. A. Onajko, 'Les relations économiques d'Héraclée du Pont avec le nord et le nord-est de la mer Noire aux époques hellénistique et romaine' (en russe), *Sov. Arkh.* 1975 86-93): les amandes en tout cas étaient transportées en sacs, ou du moins en récipients périssables, dans l'épave de Kyrénia (344).

2. Il me paraît invraisemblable que Rhodes, par exemple, ait abondamment exporté des amphores vides à Alexandrie ou en mer Noire, comme l'imaginent S. M. Sherwin-White, *Ancient Cos* (1978) 241 ou A. Sadurska, 'Timbres amphoriques de Mirmeki', dans J. Irmscher et D. B. Shelov, *Griechische Städte und einheimische Völker des Schwarzmeergebietes* (1961) 110. Même dans les grands centres importateurs devait normalement exister une production locale d'amphores – à laquelle on ne s'est guère intéressé et qui reste le plus souvent difficile à identifier. Cela ne veut cependant pas dire, comme on le verra ci-dessous, qu'il n'ait pas existé de marchés *locaux* d'amphores vides, neuves ou de récupération.

3. Sur sa personnalité, voir les articles de A. I. Meljukova, D. D. B. Shelov et Yu. G. Vinogradov dans B. N. Grakov, *L'âge du fer ancien* (1977) 203-13. L'essentiel de ses publications est constitué par son étude des timbres de Sinope: *Les timbres céramiques grecs à noms d'astynomes* (1928). Mais sa thèse (1939) sur *L'emballage timbré de la Grèce antique à l'époque hellénistique comme source pour l'histoire de la production et du commerce*, ainsi que son *corpus* des timbres céramiques trouvés en Union Soviétique (*IOSPE* III), sont malheureusement restés inédits et ne sont connus en Occident qu'à travers l'usage qu'en ont fait ses successeurs.

4. Voir essentiellement, en dernier lieu, sa publication des 'timbres amphoriques grecs' de l'Ilot de la Maison des Comédiens (*Expl. arch. Dèlos* 27 (1970) en collaboration avec M. Savvatianou-Pétropoulakou), ainsi que son opuscule *Amphoras and the ancient wine trade* (rev. ed., 1979).

5. Cf. H. P. Isler, 'Bolli d'anfora e documenti affini degli scavi di Monte Iato', *Misc. E. Manni* 4 (1980) 1215. La situation à cet égard ne ferait probablement qu'empirer si l'on entreprenait de sacrifier les *corpus* imprimés aux banques de données informatisées (ce qui n'exclut pas un 'bon' usage de celles-ci).

6. M. I. Finley, *The ancient economy* (1973) 33.

7. Je dois la traduction de certains travaux en langue russe à V. Grace et d'autres à ma femme.

8. Article à paraître dans *BCH* 106 (1982).

9. Y. Garlan, 'Chronique', *BCH* 102 (1978) 807; 'Koukos. Données nouvelles pour une nouvelle interprétation des timbres amphoriques thasiens', *Thasiaca, Suppl.* 5 au *BCH* 103 (1979) 228-9.

10. V. Grace, *Newsletter, American Research Centre in Egypt 1966* 1-5.

11. C'est l'impression que l'on retire (car aucun chiffre n'est donné) d'une liste publiée par M. Lazarov des amphores thasiennes des IVe-IIIe siècles importées en Bulgarie-Roumanie: 'Le commerce de Thasos avec la côte thrace du Pont à l'époque préromaine', *Actes du IIe Congrès int. de Thracologie, Bucarest 1976* 2 (1980) 171-87.

12. J'en présente un compte rendu détaillé dans *DHA* 7 (1982).

13. I. Glodariu, *Dacian trade with the Hellenistic and Roman world*(1976) 12 et 66; C. Muşeţeanu, N. Conovici et A. Atanasiu, 'Contribution au problème de l'importation des amphores grecques dans le sud-est de la Munténie', *Dacia* n.s. 22 (1978) 190.

14. C. Museteanu *et al.* (n. 13) 192-7.

15. 'Stamped handles of commercial amphoras', *Excavations at Nessana (Auja Hafir, Palestine)*, Ed. H. Dunscombe Colt 1 (1962) 108-9.

16. 'Stamped amphora handles from the Delian temple estates', *Stud. D. M. Robinson* 2 (1953) 127-34.

17. M. Debidour, 'Réflexions sur les timbres amphoriques thasiens', *Thasiaca* (1979) 269-314.

18. Voir en dernier lieu Y. Garlan, 'Les timbres amphoriques thasiens. Bilan et perspectives de recherche', *Annales* 1982.

19. 'Les timbres céramiques d'Héraclée du Pont' (en russe), *Num. i epigr.*, 5 (1965) 18.

20. Cf. Ph. Gauthier dans *Numismatique antique. Problèmes et méthodes* (1975) 169.

21. V. Eftimie, 'Imports of stamped amphorae in the lower Danubian regions and a draft Rumanian corpus of amphora stamps', *Dacia* n.s. 3 (1959) 206 et 209-11; V. Canarache, *Importul amforelor stampilate la Istria* (1957) 388-90; M. Gramatopol et Gh. Poenaru Bordea, *Amphora stamps from Callatis and South Dobrudja* (1970) 144-6; I. Glodariu (n. 13) 74-7.

22. Isler (n. 5) 1228.

23. Voir Garlan (n. 12) sur Brashinsky.

6. THE GRAIN TRADE AND GRAIN SHORTAGES IN THE HELLENISTIC EAST*

'When, in the Greek world enlarged through the conquests of Alexander, men moved away from agriculture and suffered from food-shortages, then came the golden age of the grain-producing countries, the era of profiteering and of gifts of grain to political ends'. Thus wrote Préaux in her magisterial study of the Ptolemaic 'royal economy', and her words echoed the views of earlier studies and are themselves echoed today.[1] However the validity of this picture is open to some doubt, in particular with reference to the maritime trade in wheat. The grain trade in the Hellenistic East is a complex subject. On the one hand the evidence for it is in aggregate abundant, though also fragmentary, of many diverse types, and scattered in numerous publications. On the other hand grain is the commodity which best illustrates the inextricable bonding of economic, political and social factors in the life of the ancient world, and the history of its trade is correspondingly intricate. A brief paper such as this must omit much of importance, but the following general considerations may perhaps serve as a possible focus for further detailed research.

The picture to be tested is that in the Hellenistic East the level of demand for imported grains in the majority of cities was on average relatively high as compared to available supplies, and that this relationship between supply and demand was to the financial (and hence political) benefit of those states or individuals who regularly had a surplus of grain available for export. In short, this picture implies that in grain-importing cities the average price of grain was relatively high. And here by 'relatively' we mean in comparison with previous and later times. Now if we had widespread and reliable statistics for grain-prices this picture could be submitted to a straightforward test. Unfortunately the one set of quite abundant data which we possess, that is the evidence from Egypt, cannot yet be used for this enquiry because of internal problems of interpretation and because of the probability that it would not anyway indicate price-levels in the East Mediterranean as a whole.[2] This lack of statistics forces us to rely largely on general considerations. Although much of interest can emerge from these, general considerations are feeble foundations on which to base statements about the relative level of grain-prices in different periods and places. This weakness obviously affects all that follows; it also applies, however, to the traditional picture of high prices.

We cannot quantify it but we cannot doubt that grain was one of the largest items of trade in the Hellenistic East both in terms of tonnage and in terms of value.[3] This follows from two general considerations. Firstly, need. Grain was the main source of nutrition for most of the population,[4] yet local shortages of grain must have been relatively frequent. Several of the cities on the Aegean islands and some cities of mainland Greece, notably Athens, simply lacked sufficient grain-land to satisfy the domestic demand for grain in any given year. Others suffered from intermittent shortages resulting from poor harvests – in many localities of modern Greece two out of seventeen years are disastrous for grain. The survival of these cities thus depended on and hence implies a considerable volume of maritime trade in grain. Secondly, the cost of transport. This was high in the ancient world, and thus particularly favoured the trade in grain as against bulkier and less manageable foodstuffs which were potential alternatives. And here it is important to note that wheat held a significant advantage over barley, since in terms of volume it had some 35% greater nutritive value and up to 100% greater cash value.[5] This last point raises the issue, which must now be examined, of the relative importance of wheat and of barley in the grain-trade of the Hellenistic East.[6]

In itself the advantage held by wheat over barley in terms of transport-costs would suggest that wheat was the main grain of maritime trade in the Hellenistic East. The comparative paucity of references in this period to imported barley is in accord with this hypothesis. To reinforce it we should demonstrate the existence – or at least the plausibility of the existence – both of supplies of wheat and of a demand for it in preference to barley. I begin with a glance at the question of supplies. To say that Egypt, including Cyrene, and the Black Sea region were the main exporters of grain in this period is not very bold. It would, however, be rash not to remember that inland Syria was also a major grain-bearing region, and that many Greek states will have had intermittent surpluses of grain for export.[7] The relative volumes of grain from these different regions available for export in an average year is not ascertainable with any exactitude, but for the Hellenistic period no-one doubts that Egypt and the Black Sea region were predominant, or that their main exported grain was wheat. Wheat, then, was the main grain available for export; whether or not supplies were sufficient in any one year it will thus have been the main grain of maritime trade in an average year.

Next comes the question of the demand for imported grains. Granted the cost and unreliability of importing grain, we would expect each city to have looked primarily to its own territory for its basic regular supply of grain, at least insofar as that territory could normally produce a sufficiency. Throughout most of the coastal areas and the islands of the East Mediterranean poor soils and the level/timing of precipitation will have been major inducements to the cultivation of barley rather than of wheat. That barley was the main grain-crop, at least in the Aegean area, is a reasonable assumption. When evidence is available it fits this picture: for instance the production of over ten times more barley than wheat in the territory of Athens is implied by the Eleusis *aparche* accounts for 329/8 B.C..[8] These factors would lead us to expect that barley was the major grain consumed in the Greek cities of the Hellenistic period; but how can this be squared with the apparent predominance of wheat in the maritime grain-trade, and, more importantly, with the apparent preference of the Greeks for wheat-bread over barley-cake/porridge which is attested by a fair spread of casual references in the literary sources?

At this point it is necessary to draw a distinction between the urban and the rural populations of a city-state. It cannot be rigorously proved, but seems in outline unexceptionable. This is that most city-dwellers bought their grain, whereas most country-dwellers produced it for themselves. Thus the latter, whatever their preference, will normally have eaten barley, while it is among the former that the preference for wheat is most likely to have been matched by actual consumption-patterns. In the case of Athens it has been plausibly argued that the urban preference for wheat developed as follows:[9] when the city population outstripped the productive capacity of its territory grain had to be imported to fill the gap; the main available grain was wheat from the Black Sea region; initial consumption of this through necessity led to its consumption through acquired preference. Thus it is probable that by the Hellenistic period a considerable proportion of the wheat imported into Athens was not merely to cover a shortfall in total local grain-production, but was imported because the city population preferred wheat to barley, the main domestic crop. Let us assume, then, for the sake of argument, that this was true of most coastal cities in the Hellenistic East: barley was the main local crop, yet the urban population preferred wheat, and would not only eat imported wheat when the local barley-crop was insufficient, but also, to a certain extent, when local barley was in ample supply. Any error in this hypothesis is in the favour of the traditional picture of high prices in the Hellenistic East.

However, if there was a genuine urban preference for wheat, why did Greek farmers not grow more wheat in place of barley? It is not possible to give a certain answer to this. Granted the normal 2:1 price-ratio of wheat to barley, which roughly reflects the ratio of production-costs (i.e. labour-input), wheat should have provided a better rate of return on the capital investment in land. However, leaving aside the question of whether an ancient Greek farmer would have thought in these terms, there is a wide range of possible circumstances which could have nullified this theoretical gain. Among them may be mentioned the risk that increased production would lead to a fall in the price of wheat, the possible unavailability of the extra labour necessary for wheat-cultivation, the dangers of competition with imported wheat from, for example, Egypt, where average yields were twice as high as in the Aegean area and production costs therefore two times lower.[10] The very existence of a standard price-ratio between wheat and barley, even if it was only a crudish official guideline which was sometimes out of tune with market-prices, implies that on the whole there was a reasonably stable market-balance both in the supply of and the demand for local barley and imported wheat.

This point can be expanded. Without casting doubt on the preference of Greek urban populations for wheat over barley, it is probable that at least the poorer citizens actually consumed a great deal of barley. If not, how does one explain that throughout the Hellenistic East the price of barley is far more frequently attested than that of wheat? It is reasonable to conclude that for the majority of city-dwellers in the Hellenistic East – and they represented the bulk of the purchasing power in the grain-trade – wheat and barley were alternative goods. Wheat may have been preferred, but it was only bought within certain financial circumstances. One strategy open to the consumer faced with a rise in the price of wheat above the level he was able or prepared to pay was to switch to the purchase of barley. Such a reaction, to give one illustration, is attested in the accounts of the *hieropoioi* on Delos for 282 B.C., when for the last three months of the year barley was purchased instead of wheat, wheat having risen in the ninth month to almost 60% over its previous average price.[11] Since most barley was locally produced and most wheat was imported, it must often have been the case that a feared or actual shortage of wheat was not accompanied by a contemporary shortage of barley. Thus rises in the price of imported wheat must often have been limited by the availability of local barley. We should remember in this context that farmers had the option, if market-conditions were favourable, of diverting barley from use as fodder to sale in the city for human consumption. In short, the availability of local barley will have acted as a brake on any short-term rise in the price of imported wheat, a fact which was not to the advantage of the exporters/suppliers of this wheat.

Against this conclusion, however, must be set the probable effects of an alternative strategy open to the average Greek city-dweller faced with an alarming rise in the price of imported wheat. The typical Greek city-state was a close-knit society of modest size, which still normally retained an autonomous domestic administration, dominated by a small very wealthy élite. The poorer victims of a feared or genuine shortage of and hence rise in the price of wheat could soon translate their grievance into mob-action, thereby pressurizing the élite to go out and seek wheat whatever the cost for sale back in the city at a subsidised price. By the Hellenistic age most cities had developed quite formal mechanisms for this type of search-purchasing.[12] One way or another the élite footed the bill, but it was a fairly low price to pay for the avoidance of riots. In fact the individual could look on it as a useful political investment – the generous benefactor in times of grain-'shortage' is a stock character in Hellenistic inscriptions. So the mob could be the grain-trader's best ally, see him as they might as a callous profiteer.

The difficulty here is to establish the relative frequency of adoption of the alternative strategies described above which were open to an urban populace faced with a sharp rise in the price of wheat. On the one hand there is reason to suspect that more barley was regularly consumed by city-dwellers than has often been supposed. On the other hand there is considerable evidence for the élite being obliged to seek extra supplies of wheat. For Athens in particular we have the long-established picture of a city constantly haunted by crises in her supply of foreign wheat. Athens takes the limelight because that is where the evidence bunches. With a peculiarly large urban population its problems may have been untypically severe, yet we may have even more fundamental doubts. If the surviving evidence seems to show the Athenian grain-supply in constant crisis, then that is largely the fault of the evidence. No axe-grinding orator, no adulatory benefactor's inscription would have wasted words on a tribute to the beneficial effects of the normal market-balance between local barley and imported wheat. The evidence is certainly crisis-oriented; sometimes its 'crises' may even have been invented. We may suspect that orators and benefactors, to further their own political interests, were on occasion not averse to promising wheat when the populace could and would have eaten barley.

To sum up what has been discussed so far, that is the various factors which probably affected the price of grain purchased in a city in years when its domestic crop was average or above-average, it would appear that there was a market-balance between local barley and imported wheat which will have tended to restrain rises in the price of wheat. Sometimes political necessity will have forced the élite to purchase foreign wheat at an inflated price; the frequency and effect of this possible phenomenon are unquantifiable, but it seems reasonable to conclude that on the whole there was not much scope for profiteering by wheat-suppliers. However, we have so far only considered the case of a real or apparent shortage of imported wheat. More important is the effect of a failure or, worse, a succession of failures of the local grain-crop. In theory, if imported wheat was readily available in sufficient quantities, this in turn will have limited the rise in the price of local barley. But this was also a particularly promising scenario for the holder of a wheat-surplus who was able to keep back his supplies and let the price rise. There can be no doubt that this sometimes occurred. A notorious example is Cleomenes, the financial controller of Egypt under Alexander the Great.[13] But domestic crop-failure and profiteering by outside suppliers must also have been features of the Classical era (and of the period of Roman domination). If the Hellenistic period is to stand out as a 'golden age' for grain-exporters we must be able to point to factors which rendered the average city more vulnerable to exploitation by grain-traders than it was in preceding or later eras. The three main areas which we should consider are the level and distribution of demand, the level and source of supplies, and the structure of the trade.

Several major elements in the question of demand have already been discussed. It has been suggested that the main grain of inter-state trade was wheat, but that demand for wheat in preference to barley was a phenomenon already established before the Hellenistic era and that this demand was on the whole limited by the continuing availability and acceptability of locally grown barley as an alternative grain. Thus even if the preference for wheat over barley became more widespread in the Hellenistic East than it had been before, it is unlikely that this led to a significant increase in the general price-level of wheat, especially, as will be argued below, since there are grounds for belief that this period saw an increase in the amount of wheat available on the international market per head of urban population. This brings us to the question of the level and distribution of population in the Hellenistic world. Again, in the absence of statistics, statements can only be impressionistic. The key issue is whether there was a rise in the total urban population which represented the market for imported grain. There were some notable examples of urban growth in the 'new' Greek world, principally Alexandria in Egypt and Antioch in Syria, but in mainland Greece the evidence points towards a certain amount of urban depopulation.[14] Thus the dominant trend appears to have been one of inter-urban migration. Overall the urban population may have grown slightly, but the evidence cannot sustain any thesis of a significant shift in the ratio or in the levels of the total urban and the total rural populations.

I turn now to the question of supplies. By the end of the II B.C. Rome had monopolised the grain-surplus of Sicily. But Sicily's reputation as a major grain-supplier to the older Greek cities may be undeserved. The chronological distribution of extant references to the import of Sicilian grain rather suggests a quite brief period of importance in the late V B.C., presumably as a result of the disruption of local grain production and trade during the Second Peloponnesian War. Conversely, the theory that Numidia began large exports of grain to the Eastern Mediterranean in the early II B.C. has been convincingly refuted by Casson.[15] It seems that on the whole there was no significant rise or fall in the Hellenistic East in the (low) level of grain imported from the Western Mediterranean. In the Classical period the single largest supplier of wheat to the Greek cities had been the Black Sea region. It is clear that it continued to export a lot of wheat in the Hellenistic period, but there is no way of quantifying whether average annual exports were larger or smaller. Therefore I tentatively assume that there was no significant rise or fall in exports from this area. It may be that the Greek conquest of and colonisation in Asia Minor and the Near East increased the amount of grain available to Greek coastal cities from the inland plains previously under Persian control,[16] but we must allow also for urban growth in these areas. Syria perhaps had some surplus wheat for export, but it is dubious whether the extension of Greek control to these areas in general made a significant difference to the volume of wheat normally available for maritime export in the Hellenistic East. Meanwhile, we may presume that some proportion of the grain traded in the Hellenistic East continued to come from the intermittent surpluses of the older Greek city-states themselves. Although the evidence is meagre, what there is does not suggest, for the areas so far considered, that there took place in the Hellenistic East any significant change in the balance between the supply of and the demand for imported wheat.

The one major grain-exporting region still to be considered is Egypt. In the Hellenistic period, indeed, it may well have equalled the Black Sea area in the volume of its exports of wheat. But the crucial question is whether there had been a change in the volume of grain-exports since the Classical period. It does seem that the foundation of Naucratis implies a Greek interest in grain from Egypt from the

VIIB.C. on,[17] but direct references to Egyptian grain are sparse in the Greek sources until the Hellenistic period. Where they do occur they normally involve special sales or gifts of grain to Greek cities from native Egyptian dynasts. In fact I suspect that less Egyptian grain reached Greek cities in the Classical than in the Archaic age. This is for two reasons. Firstly, the Persian annexation of Egypt. When supplies were not disrupted by revolts and their repression, much of the surplus must have been monopolised by the Persians for their own uses. Secondly, the then prevalent wheat in Egypt, known locally as *olyra*, was a husked emmer-wheat (*triticum dicoccum*), which was more difficult to mill and not well-suited to the production of the white bread which the city-dwelling Greeks had now come to prefer, and for which supplies of bread-wheat had become increasingly available from the Black Sea region. It would thus seem that it was under the early Ptolemies that Egypt became a major regular exporter of grain to the Greek cities.

It should be noted that the picture of increased grain-exports from Egypt under the Ptolemies does not necessarily imply that they had perceived an unsatisfied demand among the cities which their grain could fill. They had a much simpler domestic motive for exportation. The Ptolemies were determined to play their part on the world stage as one of the most powerful successor-dynasties of Alexander. To do this they needed, amongst other things, silver, iron, wood, Greek mercenaries, horses, and luxury items for the conspicuous consumption of the court.[18] All these had to be acquired from outside Egypt, and the single largest commodity which the Ptolemies could export in return was precisely grain. Of necessity the Ptolemies had to export grain, whether a favourable market for it existed or not. Indeed I would suggest, on the basis of two observations, that the market was not favourable. One observation relates to the structure of the grain-trade, to which I will return in a moment; the other concerns the replacement of *triticum dicoccum* (*olyra*) by *triticum durum*, the standard naked bread-wheat of the Greek world. *Triticum durum* may have been first introduced into Egypt by the Persians, but its rise to dominance occurred primarily under the first two Ptolemies.[19] Royal promotion of this change is attested; so is native resistance. The success of the Ptolemies must in large measure be attributed to the backing of their Greek settlers, who doubtless preferred the 'new' wheat. But, despite the need to feed Alexandria, much of this wheat was destined for foreign export. If grain-supplies in the Greek world were on the whole barely sufficient and if genuine shortages were frequent, why did the Ptolemies simply not export the traditional and more prolific *olyra*? A Greek who ate barley will not have snubbed emmer-wheat. I suggest that the efforts made by the Ptolemies to spread the cultivation of *triticum durum* in Egypt imply that the average annual supply of local barley and imported wheat in most *poleis* was already adequate, that the increased grain-exports from Egypt represented a slight surplus on the total market, and that the Ptolemies were obliged to export *triticum durum* because whereas their potential customers might buy this in preference to local barley they would not have bought *olyra.*

We thus come to the topic of the structure of the grain-trade in the Hellenistic East. It is generally and with good reason agreed that this trade was dominated by independent small-scale merchants. In the case of Egyptian wheat these were usually Rhodians; indeed the Rhodians lived largely off the Egyptian trade, according to Diodorus.[20] If wheat had been in heavy demand throughout the Eastern Mediterranean, and if prices had in consequence been consistently high, we would have reason to be surprised that the Ptolemies, who had pretensions to being a major maritime power, made almost no effort to distribute and market their wheat themselves. However, as Préaux pointed out long ago,[21] the Ptolemies will have applied the same criterion to the exportation of wheat as they did to all other types of revenue – where there was risk, they shifted it onto private entrepreneurs. It will have made good sense for the Ptolemies to sell most of their wheat at Alexandria to individual merchants and to leave them the hazards of storms, piracy and satiated markets. The merchants, after all, were forced to buy. No cargo meant no possibility of profit, and hence no livelihood. It could be objected that this makes it hard to understand why merchants bought wheat from Egypt and how they made a profit on it (and Rhodes undoubtedly prospered). The simple answer is that small-scale merchants were far more flexible than a Ptolemaic grain-fleet could ever have been. Even if on average prices were not high, there could be considerable fluctuation in any one year around the average price,[22] which gave ample scope for making great profits or great losses. The small cargo of an individual merchant would not have greatly depressed a favourable price-level in a city, whereas he could have counteracted the risks of a low price-level by dealing simultaneously in other commodities. The tensions between cities and grain-merchants probably stemmed largely from the stratagems which the latter had to adopt to make satisfactory profits in a difficult market.

Most studies of the Hellenistic world end with a reference to 'the coming of Rome'. As regards the grain-trade, the key change was Rome's monopolisation of the Egyptian wheat-surplus from 30 B.C. on. The probable effects were neatly formulated by Casson:[23] 'If we assume that during the Republic this much grain ... was kept on the eastern market, the ineluctable conclusion is that the conversion of Egypt into a Roman province brought in its wake a tremendous economic dislocation both in the east and the west. It would mean the loss to the former of its chief source of supply. And ... there should conversely be a sudden glut of grain in the west. Yet clearly this did not happen'. His solution was to conjecture that Rome had been obtaining wheat from Egypt for a long time before 30 B.C.. This conjecture has been criticised, though not disproved, from the Roman evidence;[24] for the Eastern Mediterranean, however, it is no solution – it would make the counter-factual economic dislocation gradual instead of sudden. The most plausible solution seems to me that Egypt's contribution to the grain-trade in the Hellenistic East was on the whole surplus to basic requirements.[25] Thus, when

Augustus cornered the Egyptian wheat-surplus, the most probable result will have been a slight rise in the price of wheat, but even this may have been offset by increased production under the *pax Romana*. In short, the fact that Rome could monopolise Egypt's wheat-surplus from 30 B.C. on without throwing the eastern grain-trade into chaos independently implies that Egyptian wheat represented a slight surplus on the grain-market in the Eastern Mediterranean.

It will by now be readily apparent that any attempt to reconstruct the main outlines of the grain-trade in the Hellenistic East is severely hampered by the almost total lack of evidence for huge areas of enquiry. Insofar, however, as it is valid to draw any conclusion, it would seem that there are several grounds for doubt that the Hellenistic era was a 'golden age' for the grain-exporting countries. The main reason is that the emergence of Egypt in the early III B.C. as a major wheat-exporter caused there to be a slight surplus on the international grain-market; this will in theory have eased the problems of supply for the Greek cities and have led to a certain fall in the average price of wheat. Even if Egyptian exports only represented say 10% of all traded grain in an average year, they should have had some restraining effect at the top end of the previous price-range. In practice, however, the consumers may not have seen any noticeable reduction in the average price of grain. The actual consumption of wheat in preference to barley may have risen to soak up the new surplus (the barley thereby released going to feed livestock); merchants could have exploited the situation to increase their own profits. Undoubtedly it was not a 'golden age' for the wheat-importing cities either. Civic institutions to ensure wheat imports continued to be necessary, above all because no city put much faith in the probity of the merchants. And the success of these institutions must often have confirmed their suspicions. There was also, finally, the problem, which deserves at least a belated acknowledgement, of the perennial warfare in the Hellenistic East. One might argue that the very fact that it was logistically possible testifies to the existence and manoeuvrability of a substantial grain-surplus. However, there must also have been diversions of grain-supplies away from cities, as well as the more direct effects of sieges, devastations and so on. Yet we still have reason to believe that when we hear of grain-shortages in the Hellenistic East we should in most cases ascribe them to transient blockages in the normal system of distribution rather than to any fundamental inadequacy of total supplies to meet total demand.

Aberdeen   DOMINIC RATHBONE

NOTES

* I owe much to discussion with P. D. A. Garnsey, P. Halstead, K. Hopkins, D. J. Thompson and T. S. Torrance.

1. C. Préaux, *L'économie royale des Lagides* (1939) 149; she refers (n. 1) to the similar conclusions of: F. Heichelheim, 'Sitos', *R.E.* Suppl. VI (1936) coll. 849-52, and M. Rostovtzeff, 'The Hellenistic World and its economic development', *Amer. Hist. Rev.* 41 (1936) 231-52. Most recently see F. W. Walbank, *The Hellenistic World* (1981) 161f.

2. Internal problems of interpretation include: 1. the depreciation of the copper coinage; 2. the unknown relationship between the open market price, penalty prices in contracts, and the government requisition price; 3. the possibility of regional variations. And although to an ancient historian the quantity of data seems immense, its randomness and gaps would not impress a statistician. The relationship of Egyptian prices to those of the East Mediterranean at large will almost certainly have been affected by the attempts of the Ptolemies to maintain a closed economy. The extant grain-prices from the accounts of the *hieropoioi* on Delos are simply too few to permit reconstruction of long-term trends.

3. Compare the 'sighting' calculations of K. Hopkins, *Conquerors and Slaves* (1978) 3 n. 6.

4. We may assume as a general rule, which can be illustrated by random local evidence, that other foods, and in particular pulses, played an important dietary role, but on the whole it was subsidiary. At any rate we never, to my knowledge, hear of a pulse-shortage disturbing an urban population, though admittedly a poor pulse-crop may have caused unrecorded hardship to peasants.

5. See, for example, G. E. Rickman, *The Corn Supply of Ancient Rome* (1980) 5; F. Heichelheim, *Wirtschaftliche Schwankungen der Zeit von Alexander bis Augustus* (1930) 51, 58f.

6. Ancient sources often make no more than a generic distinction between 'wheat' and 'barley' although different varieties of both were recognised; in the context of these general considerations there is no great advantage in trying to impose a preciser categorisation.

7. On the doubts about supplies from Sicily and Africa see p. 50 below.

8. *IG* II.2, 1672, ll. 263-299. Note that this is another example of a 2:1 price-ratio for wheat to barley.

9. L. Gernet, 'L'approvisionnement d'Athènes en blé au Ve et au IVe siècle', *Mélanges d'Histoire Ancienne* (1909), 271-391.

10. It is also not impossible that the standard of living of peasant cultivators in Egypt and Syria was lower than that of Greek rural populations; this would have lowered production costs further.

11. *IG* XI.2, 158, ll. 37-50. The price of a *medimnos* of wheat fluctuated as follows: Lenaion 7*dr.*, Hieros 6*dr.* 3*ob.*, Galaxion 6*dr.*, Artemision 4*dr.* 3*ob.*, Thargelion 6*dr.* 5*ob.*, (Panemos and Hekatombaion: no purchases), Metageitnion 7*dr.*, Bouphonion 10*dr.*.

12. See Jameson (in this volume).

13. Ps.-Dem. 56.7-10; ps.-Arist., *Oec.* 2.33f (=1352a-b).

14. For mainland Greece we move from Isocrates' hint (*Philippus* 121f) at overpopulation in 346 B.C. to Polybius' claims (36.17.5-10) of *apaidia* and *oliganthropia* some two hundred years later. M. Rostovtzeff, *The Social and Economic History of the Hellenistic World* (1941) 623-5 thought the evidence justified talk of 'race suicide'; for a more cautious assessment see Walbank (n. 1) 165-7. On the probable population decline at Athens in the later IV B.C. see A. W. Gomme, *The Population of Athens in the Fifth and Fourth Centuries B.C.* (1933) 18f.

15. L. Casson, 'The grain trade of the Hellenistic world', *TAPhA* 85 (1954) 168-87 (see 176-8).

16. An important text here, of which the economic significance is a matter of dispute, is the letter from Antigonus I to Teos; C. B. Welles, *Royal Correspondence*, no. 3.

17. See, for example, Bravo (in this volume).

18. The list of imports is drawn from Préaux (n. 1) 433.

19. On this agricultural revolution see D. J. Crawford, 'Food: tradition and change in Hellenistic Egypt', *World Archaeology* 11 (1979) 136-46, espec. 137-40, with bibliography.

20. Diod. Sic. 20.81.4. On the more general importance of Rhodes in the grain-trade see Casson (n. 15).

21. Préaux (n. 1) 150f.

22. For example, in the first eight months of 282 B.C. on Delos (before the dramatic price-rise in the ninth month), the attested price of wheat per *medimnos* fluctuated between 4*dr.* 3*ob.* and 7*dr.*, a range of 2*dr.* 3*ob.*, equivalent to almost 40% of the average price of 6*dr.* 2*ob.* (see n. 11 for details).

23. Casson (n. 15) 183.

24. See, for example, R. Meiggs, *Roman Ostia* (2nd ed; 1973) 472f (note C); his main argument is the silence of Cicero. As regards the hypothetical glut in the West, one could point to the continuing expansion of Rome and the needs of the newly organised standing army.

25. It might be claimed that Augustus increased Egyptian wheat-output through the employment of his army on repairs to the irrigation-system. But the time and numbers available cannot have produced such dramatic results. Maintenance of the irrigation-system was a constant necessity.

7. FAMINE IN ROME

Introduction

The first concern of inhabitants of the ancient world was how to feed themselves and their dependants.[1] The Mediterranean is a dry zone with a high interannual variation of rainfall. Crop failures are frequent and inevitable, and small producers have to be resilient to survive. This was especially true of ancient peasants, who lived in a world which knew few varieties of grain, where technology was backward, transport facilities underdeveloped and famine relief organizations non-existent.

Climate apart, the peasant's main enemy was the powerful outsider. It is a defining characteristic of the peasantry that it is subject to political and economic exploitation.[2] The seat of exploitation in the ancient world was normally the city, that community of non-producers which exercised political, administrative and financial hegemony over the adjacent countryside (cf. Galen 6.749ff.).

This is not a general account, even in outline, of food crises in the Roman world, but rather a case-study of food crisis in the best-known, largest and most exploitative of all the urban agglomerations in antiquity.[3] In its heyday Rome drew tribute in cash and kind from the entire Mediterranean world, not to mention rents from the properties it had taken over and directly controlled, for the benefit of the governing class, bureaucracy, army and the three quarters of a million to a million inhabitants of the city itself. There were, however, periodic food crises in Rome. They are best documented (for our evidence is inevitably patchy) for the early Republic,[4] the period from 75 B.C. to A.D. 70, and the second half of the fourth century A.D. Are we to infer, then, that the Roman state was unable (or unwilling) to protect the inhabitants of the city from hunger and starvation? This paper addresses itself to this question, the efficacy of the food-supply system of the city of Rome. For the purposes of this paper 'food-supply system' is shorthand for 'grain-supply system' and 'food crisis' for 'grain crisis'. A comprehensive survey of the Roman diet is beyond the scope of this paper. Grain was in any case its main element, and Roman governments distributed no other foodstuffs on a regular basis until the turn of the second century A.D. The evidence, even for grain supply and distribution in Rome, is uneven and fragmentary, providing for example a fuller picture of Rome after 123 B.C. than prior to 123 B.C. That is to say, the picture becomes tolerably clear only once some kind of public food-distribution system has been established. Thus no satisfactory comparative analysis is possible between, for example, middle and late Republic.

I use 'food crisis' in preference to 'famine' to describe the phenomenon under investigation, because it covers a broader range of cases. It is above all the multifarious nature of the phenomenon under discussion – for each food crisis was an individual event, having its own particular characteristics – which makes any general evaluation difficult.

An obvious first step is to explore the language of food crisis, to see, for example, whether it helps us distinguish between crises that were relatively grave and crises that were relatively mild. In 57 B.C. there were food riots in Rome. But according to Cicero, although prices were high, there was no severe hunger: *praesens caritas et futura fames* (*de domo* 11). The authors, Cicero included, rarely make such clear distinctions. *Fames* is not always reserved for the hunger that borders on starvation, and food crises are frequently represented as grave when internal evidence suggests that they were not. For example, Tiberius in A.D. 32 was faced with a 'severe food shortage' (*gravitate annonae*) and popular demonstrations that stopped just short of riot (*seditiones*). But he positively refused to take any emergency steps. There is no suggestion that his behaviour was irresponsible (Tac. *Ann.* 6.13). More generally, we find that food crises often appear to have been recorded not because they were in themselves catastrophic, but because, for example, a superstitious people ascribed them religious significance as portents, or because they gave rise to important social and political events, or because they illustrate the virtues or vices of an emperor, or the patriotism of a magistrate or private benefactor.

If therefore we are to produce a differentiated account of food crisis in Rome, we must look beyond the often quite opaque language of food crisis to the narrative, where one exists, and we must examine such factors as the cause or context of food crisis, its duration, the behaviour of ordinary people and the response of governments.[5] Of these factors the temporal one can be dealt with briefly. A succession of bad or mediocre harvests will have had a more devastating effect than a single one, whether we are considering a rural or an urban context. Surplus stocks will last only so long. The panic in Rome in A.D. 51 followed a series of droughts (*assiduas sterilitates*), which left the state granaries almost empty (Suet. *Claud.* 18.2; Tac. *Ann.* 12.43). At the other extreme, some shortages in Rome have a suspicious tendency to disappear almost overnight, for example those of 67 B.C. and 57 B.C. leading to Pompey's appointments against the pirates and to a *cura annonae*, respectively.[6]

Causes

Any general account of the causes of food crisis in the Mediterranean must start from climatic irregularities, which meant that grain production was subject to considerable fluctuations. Such irregularities were a fact of life, and are mentioned by the historical sources only if they were repeated from year to year, or if they combined with other factors to transform what was essentially a minor misfortune into a major catastrophe.

One such factor was plague or epidemic disease. The historical sources, as one might expect, do not bring out the complex relationship between food shortage and epidemic disease. As against those cases where food shortage was chronologically prior, leading through the consumption of poor food-substitutes to sickness and death, one can set others where the relationship worked the other way: where epidemic disease, not originating in malnutrition, killed off farmers (and cattle), cultivation was interrupted or reduced, and food crisis followed. The historical sources sometimes suggest a chronological relationship, but have little or nothing to contribute on the nature of the particular disease (e.g. Dio 54.1.1-2).

Warfare and its effects were more easily understood. War induced food crisis by disrupting agriculture and cutting supply lines. In the simplest and most extreme case, the city, its population swelled through an influx of rural dwellers seeking security, might itself come under siege. However, after the early period down to the siege and sack of Rome by the Gauls in the early fourth century B.C., if we except Hannibal's march on Rome in 211-10 B.C. (cf. Polyb. 9.11[a]), the city was not threatened by foreign foes for more than six centuries. Rome's granaries abroad, however, were vulnerable. A food crisis of about 138 B.C., briefly alluded to by Valerius Maximus (7.3), is probably related to the First Sicilian Slave Revolt, assuming that began in the previous year. Nomadic incursions into Africa Proconsularis may have contributed to the food crises of A.D. 6 and 19 (Dio 55.28.4; Tac. *Ann.* 3.20). Again, the transport of grain from the provinces to Rome might be disrupted by piratical activity, such as precipitated or aggravated the food crisis of 67 B.C.

But the relation between war and food shortage has other dimensions. Prolonged warfare placed an extra burden on the state's resources of food. The consul Aurelius Cotta in Sallust (*Hist.* 2.47.6-7) conveys this message to the rioters of 75 B.C., a year of food crisis in Rome. Cotta cites specifically the Sertorian war in Spain, the threat of Mithridates in the East where two armies were stationed, enemies in Macedonia and pirates everywhere. Again, we may conjecture that the food crisis which began in A.D. 6 (Dio 55.26) was the more severe because of the urgent need to divert resources to Illyria to combat the revolt which flared up in that year. Roman armies could not always or in all periods live entirely off the localities where they were stationed or which lay in their path.

To foreign war we can add civil war (and the categories overlap). Sextus Pompeius in Sicily (42 B.C. ff.), Clodius Macer in Africa (A.D. 68), and Gildo in Africa (late fourth century) are concrete and familiar examples of the disruptive effect of civil war on the food supply of the capital. In general, emperors and would-be emperors were very conscious of the strategic importance of the grain-exporting provinces (e.g. Tac. *Ann.* 2.59; *Hist.* 3.48).

In addition to warfare and political upheaval, bad weather at sea might interrupt the flow of grain to Rome. Shipments normally took place from the late spring to the early autumn, the safe period of navigation. When stocks were low at the end of the closed season, the prompt arrival of the fleet from North Africa was crucial. Its lateness in A.D. 359 and again in 384 caused panic in the city (Amm. 19.10; Symm. *Rel.* 3.15ff.; 18.2). St Paul travelled on two Alexandrian grain ships: one went down with its cargo at Malta, the other wintered there and was several months late arriving at Puteoli (Acts 27.6ff.). In general it can be assumed that shipwrecks and the dumping or spoilage of cargo were regular occurrences on the grain routes. Claudius' offer to merchants to carry the expense of losses due to storms was a very significant concession (Suet. *Claud.* 18).

Finally, the grain supply and grain prices might be artificially controlled for the economic and political advantage of individuals. Such manipulation of the market only became dangerous when grain was for other reasons in short supply. In 67 B.C. the grain-ships were intercepted by pirates and prices rose. Pompey was appointed to put an end to the pirate menace once and for all, and on that day the price collapsed. A plausible interpretation of these events is that grain that had been held back was now released in haste before regular grain shipments resumed and the bottom fell out of the market. The speculators, to the extent that they aggravated the shortage, did Pompey a good turn. There are signs that they were active in the following decade, again to the advantage of Pompey. When Cicero went into exile about 20 March, 58 B.C., the price of grain was high. It was high again when his recall was under debate in the senate, but on the day it was approved, 4 August, 57 B.C., the price fell. It rose again in the month that ensued before his return on 4 September. There were riots, and cheap grain was demanded of Cicero. Cicero responded by proposing Pompey's *cura annonae* on 7 September, and the price fell. Clodius said at the time of Pompey's appointment that the shortage had been laid on by Pompey, and Cicero does not succeed in banishing this suspicion from our minds, especially as he virtually admits that grain had been held back as late as September (to increase the pleasure with which Romans would greet the grain when it eventually came!).

Such events were not likely to recur under the Principate.[7] Tiberius' hard line in A.D. 32 may however indicate that he was prepared to tolerate mild speculation on the part of traders (Tac. *Ann.* 6.13), and indeed imperial officials may themselves have indulged in it in disposing of surplus stocks of state grain (cf. Tac. *Ann.* 14.50).[8]

Of these sundry causes of food crisis, war was potentially the most damaging, in that it was capable of producing not simply dearth, but outright starvation, notably in the context of a siege when one side was effectively cut off from external supplies. Livy describes the crisis of 492-1 B.C., a peace-time crisis, as having produced a level of suffering experienced by those under siege: 'fames qualis clausis solet' (2.34.1). In the fact that war-induced famine was common in early Roman history we have the beginnings of a contrast between early Rome and later periods, in terms of the severity of the food crises suffered. A consideration of other aspects of the narratives of food crisis, and first, the response of the people, will enable us, among other things, to develop this point.

The above catalogue does not furnish a general explanation of food crisis in Rome. Rome did not stand still, demographically or politically; food crises did not follow one or even several repeating patterns. To say that an interplay of natural and human causes was a regular feature of food crisis is not a bold assertion, but it does at least provide a starting point for the construction of more ambitious hypotheses. One might argue, for example, with respect to the city of Rome, that its food supply was essentially a logistical matter, a problem of distributing stocks of grain which were already in principle obtainable in sufficient quantity – because Rome could draw from the whole Mediterranean – and harvest failure was never likely to be sufficiently widespread to put the people of Rome at jeopardy. It would follow that food crises in Rome were caused not by a lack of available food but by a man-made failure to move it where it was needed.

The behaviour of the people

Under this head may be listed popular complaint (ranging from peaceful protest to riot), consumption of strange foodstuffs, emigration, exposure or sale of children, suicide and death by starvation. Most of these may be taken as symptoms of severe hunger. They crop up typically in the context of war, and hardly at all after the early Republic. This must be significant, even if allowance is made for our literary sources' limited interest in the situation of ordinary people. Dio's brief notice (48.18.1) to the effect that many died in the city following Sextus Pompeius' blockade of the city is exceptional. It can be assumed that the mortality rate among the urban poor increased whenever, for example, epidemic disease was associated with food shortage, and that the sources were simply not concerned to place this on record. On the other hand, such catastrophes appear to have been rare in Roman history after the early period.

However, popular protest is attested with relative frequency, and must be given separate consideration. Dionysius under 493-2 B.C. represents rioting as an alternative to eating strange foods, for the hungry. By strange foods is meant not alternative foods, but items that were, properly speaking, not food at all: roots, herbs, leaves, grass and the like. The people of Casilinum, besieged by Hannibal, ate all the animals they could find, rats included, dug out every kind of plant and root from the bank beneath the wall, and chewed thongs and hides stripped off shields after softening them in hot water (Livy 23.19.2ff.; cf. 23.30.2).

Riots *could* be a last resort of desperate people, as is indicated for example by the accounts in Dio and Appian of events in Rome in 42-36. However, fear of starvation rather than starvation itself might be sufficient to generate crowd violence. In A.D. 51 Claudius was hustled in the forum. The mob pelted him with crusts, however, not stones, and we are told that there was still grain in the state granaries, even if only enough for fifteen days (Tac. *Ann.* 12.43). In late antique Rome, a delay in the arrival of the grain fleet from Africa was liable to set the people on the rampage (e.g. Amm. 19.10). They were not yet starving: they anticipated starvation.

There is no necessary correlation between popular protest and the level of suffering that lies behind it. A sudden price rise might in itself be sufficient to set in motion a riot having its origin in, and drawing its strength from, deeper social or political discontents. The riots of 57 B.C. were of that order. A food crisis, characterised by *caritas* but not *inopia* or *fames*, at least according to Cicero, was engineered, or aggravated, by Pompey's friends, and provoked a riot which itself appears to have been primarily a political event.

A riot in the reign of Augustus took a similar form. In fact, Dio's accounts of the riots of 57 and 22 B.C. run closely parallel. In both cases the senate in session was besieged by an angry crowd which threatened to burn the building and those within it (39.4.2; 54.1.3). The severity of the 22 B.C. crisis is hard to gauge. Plague and flooding are part of the background, and according to Augustus' own account there was a very serious grain shortage (*penuria frumenti summa*: *RG* 5); on the other hand, he goes on to state that he put an end to the crisis 'in a few days'. We are left with the impression that the scale of the riots in 22 was related to the political uncertainty that followed the changes of 23, and in particular the fear that Augustus by giving up the consulship had abdicated direct responsibility for the welfare of the people of Rome. The risk of rioting at this level in the context of food crisis was considerably reduced once the emperor had taken charge of the food supply, which he did precisely in 22. There is no suggestion in Dio's account of the far more serious crisis of A.D. 6 that Augustus was driven to take energetic measures by mob action (55.26).[9]

Non-violent protest was another matter. In A.D. 32 following a price rise the people raged against the emperor in the theatre for several days with unusual insolence, almost crossing the border between protest and riot (*iuxta seditionem ventum*: Tac. *Ann.* 6.13). Demonstration, but not riot, was tolerated by emperors. It did not threaten the regime, at most reminding the emperor, who was frequently present, of his obligation to feed the people. It took place in a controlled environment, normally the theatre or the hippodrome, and it was essentially non-violent.[10] However, this distinction between demonstration and riot may be less valid in other periods of Roman history, and in any case it is an uncertain guide to the condition of the people in any particular food crisis.

The response of government

Dio writes under A.D. 6: 'There was also a severe famine. In consequence of this famine, the gladiators, and the slaves who were for sale, were banished to a distance of 100 miles, Augustus and the other officials dismissed the greater part of their retinues, a recess of the courts was taken, and senators were permitted to leave the city and proceed wherever they pleased. Moreover, ex-consuls were appointed to have oversight over the grain and bread supplies, so that only a fixed quantity should be sold to each person. Augustus, to be sure, gave free of cost to those who were receiving doles of corn as much again in every case as they were getting; but when even that did not suffice for their needs, he forbade even the holding of public banquets on his birthday' (Dio 55.26.1-3; cf. Suet. *Aug.* 42.3).

Augustus' birthday was September 23. If food was so short right at the end of the sailing season, the emergency measures really did have point. And they *were* emergency measures: even the doubling of the corn dole, while indicating that the public granaries were not empty, shows also that there must have been a dearth of corn *on the market*. The seriousness of the crisis becomes clear when we look for comparable measures: there are virtually none. The removal of people away from the city is not attested again before the late fourth century. The standard response of governments in all periods was that of Claudius in A.D. 51, or that of Augustus in B.C. 22, to seek additional stocks of grain.

On the other hand, both those crises stimulated the emperors concerned into taking decisions which had *long-term* significance. Augustus took the *cura annonae*, and thereafter emperors were personally responsible for the corn-supply. The appointment of a *praefectus annonae*, from the closing years of Augustus' reign, was a symbol of the imperial commitment. Claudius set in motion the construction of better harbour facilities at Ostia, and introduced concessions for private traders and shipowners to encourage them to engage in the task of importing grain into Rome.[11] These incidents prompt several general questions. What long-term arrangements were made for the feeding of Rome, how comprehensive were they, when were they introduced and how if at all were the various developments related to particular food crises? These are large topics, – concerning no less than the character of the Roman food-supply and -distribution system, and the manner, momentum, and causes of its growth –, and I can only aspire to a brief treatment of them now.

I note first that the system was a long time coming. Looked at schematically, the development runs like this:

1. The flow of regular tax-grain and rent-grain began in the last decade of the third century. Presumably better public storage facilities were constructed then or soon afterwards. Gaius Gracchus' actions in 123 show that they proved inadequate.[12]

2. Subsidized grain became available on a regular basis from 123 B.C.

3. The threat to the food-supply represented by the pirates was not finally dealt with until 67 B.C.

4. Distribution of free grain began in 58 B.C.

5. There was no permanent official for the food-supply until Augustus established the *praefectura annonae*, late in his reign.

6. The harbour facilities at Ostia, improved under Claudius and Nero, were not adequate before Trajan.

This brief outline omits a number of supplementary changes and regulations, but it also passes over all the half-measures, ad hoc adjustments, and of course omissions and failures to act – not to mention steps backward, such as the lex Octavia (of the 90s?) which reduced the number of recipients of state grain, and the Sullan law which abolished the system.[13]

Secondly, the service provided for the people of Rome was relatively rudimentary, the protection it afforded only partial. Numbers of recipients were small until the law of 62 B.C. associated with Cato, and they were always in the minority. Again, the amount of grain dispensed, though more than enough for each recipient as an individual, was less than the basic food requirement of a family of four. Some dole-recipients therefore had to buy grain on the open market. Moreover, the grain-market, as far as can be seen, was more or less unregulated. We do not find, as we do in medieval Europe, an elaborate system of regulations aimed at protecting the consumer and preventing profiteering.[14] The evidence for state intervention of any kind is thin. There is no hint, in the sources of the Principate, for example, of an equivalent (in grain) to the late imperial *panis fiscalis*, subsidized bread, coexisting with *panis gradilis*, free bread.[15] In the matter of prices we hear only of an occasional maximum price for grain, as in A.D. 19 and 64 (Tac. *Ann.* 2.87; 15.39). Augustus, it appears, preferred the grand gesture, the furnishing of grain by special distribution. In A.D. 6 he took the drastic step of rationing grain.

This brings us to my third point, which concerns attitude and motivation. Augustus' reaction to the crisis of A.D. 6 was to entertain the idea of abolishing the distribution system altogether (Suet. *Aug.* 42). He retained it, out of political considerations. He had however (in 2 B.C.) reduced the number of recipients from about one-third of the population to about one-seventh. On the face of it his attitude was not much more progressive than that of conservative Republican senators such as Cicero who disliked the distribution in principle. For that matter, it would be naive to suggest that the *champions* of the system, those who established it over a long period of time, were moved primarily by sympathy for the urban poor.[16] In this connection it is significant that there is no close correlation between the institutional changes involved in the introduction and development of the supply and distribution system and the incidence of serious food shortage. In particular, food crisis does not form part of the context of the laws of Gracchus, Cato and Clodius, as far as we can tell. Of course one can always fall back on the assertion that food crisis forms part of the *general* background, but that is less solid ground on which to base an argument for a social welfare motive behind these developments.

Conclusion

One might be tempted to carry the critique of the system of supply and distribution one stage further. It might be suggested that if the historical sources had not systematically excluded the sufferings of the urban poor from their narratives, and had been prepared to document deaths by starvation and disease (and also endemic malnutrition), the system would appear in an even less impressive light. This argument however can be taken too far. The sources, one might say, do not merely fail to report catastrophe, they do not allow us to infer catastrophe. The food crises they report were *relatively* mild. Only in the annuals of early Rome is epidemic disease regularly linked with food shortage in the early narratives; people die, eat strange things and jump into the Tiber; war-induced food crisis, generally more serious than peacetime crisis, was common. But these happenings predate the development of the institutions I have been describing.

In short, the system of supply and distribution developed for Rome took the edge off the suffering of the populace. I claim no more for it than this, nor do I ascribe to those who introduced and operated it any higher motive than that of maintaining a docile people.

Cambridge   PETER GARNSEY

NOTES

1. I make no attempt to provide a full bibliography for the matters treated in this paper, and I leave aside completely literature from other historical periods. The following books are particularly to be recommended: D. van Berchem, *Les distributions de blé et d'argent à la plèbe romaine sous l'empire* (1939); P. A. Brunt, *Italian Manpower, 225 B.C. - A.D. 14* (1971), esp. 376ff., 703ff.; A. Cameron, *Bread and Circuses: the Roman Emperor and his People* (1974); H. Pavis d'Escurac, *La préfecture de l'annone: service administratif impérial d'Auguste à Constantin* (1976); K. S. Gapp, *Famine in the Roman World from the founding of Rome to the time of Trajan*, Ph.D. Thesis Princeton, 1934; A. R. Hands, *Charities and Social Aid in Greece and Rome* (1968); R. MacMullen, *Enemies of the Roman Order* (1966), App. A; J. R. Rea, *The Oxyrhynchus Papyri*, vol. 40 (1973); G. E. Rickman, *The Corn Supply of Ancient Rome* (1980); H. Schneider, *Wirtschaft und Politik: Untersuchungen zur Geschichte der späten römischen Republik* (1974); P. Veyne, *Le pain et le cirque* (1976).

For the late Empire, which I largely omit, see A. Cameron, *Circus Factions* (1976); J.-M. Carrié, 'Les distributions alimentaires dans les cités de l'empire romain tardif', *MEFR* 87 (1975), 995-1101; A. H. M. Jones, *Later Roman Empire* (1966) 695ff.; H. P. Kohns, *Versorgungskrisen und Hungerrevolten im spätantiken Rom* (1961); L. Ruggini, *Economia e società nell'Italia annonaria* (1961); E. Tengstrom, *Bread for the People, Studies of the corn-supply of Rome during the late Empire* (1974).

2. T. Shanin, 'The Nature and Logic of the Peasant Economy', *Jl. Peas. Stud.* 1 (1973) 63-80.

3. The only detailed account is by Gapp (n. 1) and regrettably unpublished. While limited in scope and objectives (and quite inadequate as a study of the Roman world, as distinct from the city of Rome), this is a sound, scholarly work, and has influenced the writing of this paper.

4. I pass over here the special problems posed by the accounts of early Rome. Those early food crises did occur (cf. Cato, *Origines* fr. 77 P) even if the detailed narratives are unreliable.

5. The last two topics are given broad treatment in P. Garnsey, 'Response of government and people to food crisis in the cities of the ancient Mediterranean (500 B.C. - A.D. 600)', *Famine in History Symposium*, Vevey, July 1981.

6. Plut. *Pomp.* 26.2, Cic. *de lege Man.* 44; *de domo* 1-32, *Att.* 4.1, *Dio* 39.9, Plut. *Pomp.* 49.4-50.2; etc.

7. The existence of the (?Augustan) lex Iulia de annona, known only from the *Digest* (48.4), need not have been decisive in this connection. There is no evidence that it was ever enforced.

8. H. Pavis d'Escurac (n. 1) 260ff. argues for regular intervention in the market by the prefect of the corn-supply.

9. After describing the measures, Dio makes brief mention of the distress caused by the food crisis, new taxes and fire, and of open discussion of revolution – but not of riot.

10. A good brief discussion in Cameron, *Bread and Circuses* (n. 1).

11. Suet. *Claud.* 18.3-4, 19; Gaius, *Inst.* 1.32c; *Dig.* 3.6 (Ulp.); P. Pomey, A. Tchernia, 'Le tonnage maximum des navires de commerce romains', *Archaeonautica* 2 (1978) 233-51, at 237-43.

12. On the food needs of Rome, sources of supply and the grain trade, I cite from the extensive literature only the following recent contributions: Pavis d'Escurac (n. 1) 166ff.; K. Hopkins, *Conquerors and Slaves* (1978) 96-99; Rickman (n. 1); J. Rougé, *Recherches sur l'organisation du commerce maritime en Méditerranée sous l'empire romaine* (1966); P. Garnsey, 'Grain for Rome', in Garnsey, Hopkins, Whittaker, edd., *Trade in the ancient economy* (1983), On the distributions, see Schneider (n. 1) 361-91; Brunt (n. 1) 376ff.; Cl. Nicolet, 'Le temple des Nymphes et les distributions frumentaires à Rome d'après des découvertes récentes', *CRAI* 1976 29-51; 'Tessères frumentaires et tessères de vote', *Mélanges Heurgon* (1976) 695-716. On individual measures, see e.g. Cl. Nicolet, 'Varron et la politique de Gaius Gracchus', *Historia* 1979 276-300; J.-M. Flambard, 'Clodius, les collèges, la plèbe et les esclaves', *MEFR* 89 (1977) 115-56, esp. 145-9; Cl. Nicolet, 'La lex Gabinia-Calpurnia de insula Delo et la loi "annonaire" de Clodius (58 av. J.C.)', *CRAI* 1980 260-92.

13. Despite H. Last, *CAH* IX 57ff., there was nothing novel about this measure of Gracchus. See, briefly, Rickman (n. 1) 46-7 (with refs.).

14. L. A. Tilly, 'The food riot as a form of political conflict in France', *Jl. Interdisc. Hist.* 2.1 (1971) 23-58, at 27ff.

15. Carrié (n. 1) 1037ff.

16. For that matter, it is worth remembering that increased corn production in Sicily, Sardinia and Campania after the Hannibalic war was turned to the feeding of Romans on service abroad as well as of residents of the city. Note in this connection the destination of the two tithes from Sicily and Sardinia in 190, 189 and 171 B.C., Livy 36.2.12ff., 50.9ff., 42.31.8. The plebs of course were not offered regular (*subsidized*) grain until 123 B.C.

17. One large question worth investigation is how far the diversion of massive stocks of grain (and other commodities) to Rome and its armies undermined the position of residents of hundreds of lesser urban communities in the empire at large, not to mention that of the vast majority of the population, namely rural dwellers. But this matter must be left for another occasion.

8. LA CÉRAMIQUE COMME INDICE DU COMMERCE ANTIQUE (RÉALITÉS ET INTERPRÉTATIONS)

1. – Que la céramique soit un instrument de mesure privilégié du commerce antique, c'est l'évidence même. Deux raisons essentielles à cela: son indestructibilité, et son rôle dans l'économie et la culture de l'Antiquité. Mais qui ne voit les risques de distorsion que ces affirmations véhiculent avec elles? L'indestructibilité de la céramique ne saurait faire oublier le poids autrement considérable de tous les indices qui ont disparu parce qu'ils étaient périssables, ou récupérables. Et l'importance que nous prêtons à la céramique doit être tempérée, lorsque nous constatons, par exemple, à la lumière de l'échantillonnage complet offert par Pompéi, que sous l'Empire le bronze et le verre rivalisaient en abondance avec la poterie 'fine'.

On peut, du reste, écrire l'histoire du commerce antique sans évoquer la céramique, comme le montre l'excellent livre de A. Mele, *Prexis ed emporie*, qui se fonde essentiellement sur des textes, lesquels sont à peu près muets sur le rôle économique de la céramique: ce n'est pas forcément souhaitable, et c'est souvent franchement impossible, faute d'autres indices. Mais le bon usage de la céramique exige que nous éliminions les à-peu-près quant aux identifications, aux datations, et – problème trop négligé – aux quantifications (quel sens y a-t-il à mettre sur le même plan, pour le bucchero étrusque, la poignée de fragments trouvés dans toute l'Espagne et les milliers de fragments trouvés sur le seul site de Saint-Blaise; ou, pour la campanienne A, les quelques tessons signalés à Rome et les quelques dizaines de tessons signalés dans chaque mètre cube fouillé sur l'oppidum gaulois de Nages?). Toute vérification approfondie que l'on se donne la peine de faire révèle avec quelle légèreté ces diverses erreurs, dont les effets finissent par se cumuler, sont acceptées et transmises.

Je chercherai donc, non pas tant à montrer que la céramique nous aide à étudier le commerce antique, qu'à suggérer avec quelle prudence elle doit être maniée, et combien sont variées les voies qu'elle ouvre à la recherche. Je centrerai mon propos sur les problèmes concernant le commerce (plutôt que l'économie en général); les 'vases-marchandises' (plutôt que les 'vases-conteneurs'); et la céramique italienne, surtout à l'époque républicaine, sans m'interdire toutefois de chercher des exemples ou des parallèles dans d'autres périodes et d'autres régions de l'Antiquité.

2. – Les modes de diffusion.

2.1. – Ne requérant ni matières premières rares, ni installations compliquées, ni techniques très élaborées, la céramique peut être faite à peu près partout. Aussi ne saurait-on trop insister sur l'incroyable dispersion des ateliers et, par conséquent, sur l'autosuffisance, pour l'essentiel, de la plupart des collectivités humaines. Il n'est guère de site antique qui ne révèle la présence d'une ou plusieurs officines de potiers. La règle générale est donc qu'une production a de fortes chances de n'être commercialisée qu'à l'intérieur d'une zone restreinte, et que les faciès céramiques des diverses régions sont extrêmement morcelés. Réduire cette réalité complexe à quelques schémas simples – simplistes – constitue l'une des principales causes d'erreur dans l'étude du commerce antique des biens de consommation courante.

Cette règle de la diffusion restreinte admet bien entendu des exceptions, parmi lesquelles peuvent figurer aussi bien des céramiques dites 'communes' que des productions de 'demi-luxe'. Il n'y a pas de différence d'échelle entre les deux catégories, du moins à l'époque romaine, car toute céramique est alors, par définition, un objet bon marché, qu'il est hors de question de considérer comme un signe de luxe. Une céramique n'est pas exportée parce qu'elle est 'belle', mais parce que, grâce à un prix particulièrement bas, elle peut rivaliser sur des marchés éloignés avec les productions locales. En somme, il faudrait inverser en une certaine mesure l'affirmation de T. Frank selon laquelle 'ancient transportation was too costly to make commerce in cheap wares profitable': c'est bien souvent parce qu'une céramique était bon marché que son commerce était profitable.

Dans un monde romain où la fabrication domestique des poteries n'existe plus, pratiquement toute poterie fait l'objet d'un commerce. Mais ce mot recouvre des réalités très diverses, sans compter quelques causes possibles d'équivoque qu'il importe de signaler préalablement, en considérant à cet effet l'antiquité classique dans son ensemble.

2.2. – Les phénomènes de diffusion différents du commerce proprement dit.

2.2.1. – *Les transports d'objets.*

Observons telle tombe d'Akrai, en Sicile, où figurent en 9 exemplaires des vases fabriqués à Capoue et qui n'ont pas été diffusés, à d'infimes exceptions près, hors de Campanie. La composition de ce mobilier funéraire a donc toutes chances de résulter d'un événement fortuit ('souvenirs' rapportés de Campanie, ou toute autre explication analogue qu'on voudrait imaginer), et de ne rien devoir au commerce. Faire figurer ce genre de trouvailles sur une carte de répartition est donc trompeur ou pour le moins ambigu.

2.2.2. – *Les traditions.*

Il s'agit de ce genre de mémoire collective qui conduit des artisans appartenant à une même ethnie à produire, quoique géographiquement très éloignés les uns des autres, des objets (par exemple des vases) très semblables entre eux, et qui faute d'un examen attentif risquent de passer pour les indices d'un commerce interrégional. C'est le cas des céramiques 'ioniennes' dans la Méditerranée nord-occidentale, des céramiques 'puniques' dans la Méditerranée sud-occidentale. Le fait de trouver à Velia et à Ampurias des vases à bandes à peu près semblables, à Solunto et à Carthage des timbres sur vernis noir à peu près identiques, n'a que peu ou rien à voir avec le commerce.

2.2.3. – *Les imitations*. Les céramiques sont en général assez faciles à imiter dans leur aspect extérieur. De fait, la littérature archéologique fourmille de mentions d'"imitations', par exemple en Gaule, par rapport aux céramiques importées de Grèce, puis d'Italie. Encore faut-il employer ce mot à bon escient, et lorsque sont remplies quelques conditions dont les deux principales sont la non-antériorité de l'imitation par rapport au modèle supposé, et ... une ressemblance incontestable.

2.2.4 – *Les transferts*. Les meilleures imitations, les plus trompeuses pour notre sujet, résultent souvent d'un transfert de main d'oeuvre (potiers émigrés rapportant ensuite certaines 'idées' dans leur région d'origine, potiers expatriés introduisant leur savoir-faire dans leur nouvelle patrie). Les grands progrès récemment accomplis dans l'étude de ce phénomène conduisent souvent à un 'ridimensionamento' des échanges commerciaux. On connaissait le cas des céramiques hellénisantes de l'Etrurie archaïque, depuis l'étrusco-corinthien jusqu'aux hydries de Caere. On peut déceler une problématique analogue derrière la prolifération des céramiques à vernis noir 'pseudo-attiques', des campaniennes 'B-oïdes' et peut-être des céramiques grises 'phocéennes', entre autres: autant de cas où la notion d'artisan itinérant, ou émigré, ou rapatrié, bat en brèche celle d'un véritable commerce.

2.2.5. – *Les succursales*. Un pas important est franchi lorsqu'un atelier délègue au loin une partie de sa force de travail afin de conquérir de nouveaux marchés grâce à la fondation d'une succursale mieux située que la maison-mère. C'est récemment qu'on en a pris conscience à propos de la sigillée 'arétine' (les guillemets s'imposent désormais), qui a essaimé d'Arezzo successivement à Pise, puis à Lyon, et sans doute dans d'autres localités de Gaule comme La Graufesenque, afin, pense-t-on, d'être mieux à même d'approvisionner les armées romaines du *limes* de Germanie. La connaissance de ce fait bouleverse nos habitudes de pensée en ce qui concerne le commerce de l'arétine. On le constate aussi, du reste, pour des ateliers de sigillée gauloise, grands (La Graufesenque) ou modestes (Luxeuil). Une fois de plus, la notion de transport *de marchandises* à grande distance se trouve ébranlée.

2.2.6. – *Les contrefaçons* sont difficiles à situer dans cette problématique: elles peuvent *a priori* se rattacher à l'une quelconque des trois situations précédentes. Limitons-nous à en constater l'existence – dont les conséquences rejoignent celles que nous venons de signaler –, depuis un atelier de Pompéi qui surmoulait des lampes en supprimant toutefois leur marque, jusqu'à des officines d'Orient ou de Lyon qui marquaient leurs vases de sigillée d'un *ARR(etinum uas)* mensonger et trompeur.

Tous ces phénomènes très divers invitent donc à la prudence: trouver à grande (ou petite!) distance l'un de l'autre deux vases semblables n'implique pas qu'il y ait eu *commerce* entre deux points, ou depuis un unique atelier vers ces deux points.

2.3 – Le commerce lui-même présente pour l'essentiel les cas de figure suivants, en fonction des quantités concernées et du rayonnement des ateliers.

2.3.1. – Diffusion, dans un rayon très réduit (de l'ordre de quelques kilomètres, rarement plus) de quantités de céramique qui peuvent être faibles ou importantes. C'est, on l'a vu, la règle générale, et l'intérêt qui se concentre sur les cas de diffusion lointaine ne doit pas faire oublier le phénomène difficile à étudier, mais essentiel, qu'est l'émiettement des productions et de leur distribution. Mentionnons le seul exemple d'une fabrique de gobelets à paroi mince du type 'Aco' implantée à Cosa et qui, malgré les mérites de ses produits, n'a pratiquement rien diffusé hors de Cosa, où elle détient en revanche une sorte de monopole: type même de ces 'petites et moyennes entreprises' qui constituent la substance de la réalité artisanale tout au long de l'Antiquité.

2.3.2. – Diffusion de quantités très faibles, mais parfois à grande distance. C'est un phénomène exceptionnel par définition, puisque la diffusion lointaine ne fait pas bon ménage avec la petite série. Le meilleur exemple en est la céramique de Calès. Répartie avec une densité du reste toute relative dans sa zone de production et en Étrurie, elle a diffusé aussi outre-mer (Gaule méridionale, Ibérie, Afrique) quelques vases si rares qu'on serait tenté de parler de transports d'objets, si l'on n'en avait trouvé des exemplaires groupés dans une épave. Mentionnons aussi certains bols à reliefs, la céramique ibérique, la céramique grise des côtes catalanes, etc. Comme il est improbable qu'un commerce autonome ait pu concerner des quantités très réduites de céramique, nous devons *a priori* voir dans ces exemples comme un signal d'alerte, ces céramiques pouvant constituer les marchandises d'accompagnement, seules perceptibles à nos yeux, de produits plus massivement exportés.

2.3.3. – Diffusion en grande quantité, mais limitée pour l'essentiel à un rayon de quelques dizaines de kilomètres: ainsi les céramiques 'de Gnathia', de grand mérite technique et artistique, mais dont la diffusion en masse, cependant, ne dépasse pas l'Apulie (ce que l'on trouve ailleurs, ici ou là, se limite à quelques unités). On doit en outre, en ce cas comme en tant d'autres analogues, poser l'hypothèse d'une nébuleuse régionale d'ateliers dont chacun aurait eu une diffusion encore plus restreinte qu'on ne l'imagine.

Nous avons là l'exemple d'une céramique trompeuse pour l'histoire économique, et par elle-même, et par l'usage qu'on en a fait. Bornons-nous ici à deux raisons. 1) Le nom de céramique 'de Gnathia', lui-même contestable, a été étendu, par un phénomène de simplification courant en céramologie, mais toujours redoutable, à toutes les autres céramiques à décor surpeint, qui abondent dans de nombreuses régions autour de 300 av.n.è.; 2) Comme en outre on prête plus d'attention à ces céramiques décorées qu'à des productions simples, on en conclut volontiers à un dynamisme remarquable de la Grande-Grèce en matière d'exportations de céramique, opinion qui repose en définitive sur des céramiques mal identifiées et dont le nombre est, de surcroît, exagéré.

2.3.4. – Diffusion en quantités importantes, pour l'essentiel dans un rayon d'une centaine de kilomètres, mais avec des prolongements plus lointains, notamment outre-mer, en quantités encore notables. C'est typiquement le cas du bucchero étrusque, de l'atelier des petites estampilles, ou de la campanienne C: toutes céramiques qui manifestement ont su opérer une percée à l'exportation, tout en fondant leur succès principalement sur un marché intérieur.

2.3.5. – Diffusion en quantités importantes, parfois immenses, à des distances aussi bien très lointaines que proches. Des exemples typiques de ces productions à marché 'mondial' sont la céramique attique à vernis noir, peut-être quelques sigillées claires, et surtout la campanienne A, produite à Naples (et aux environs?) aux IIe-Ier s. av.n.è.

2.3.6. – Considérons ce tableau, certes schématique, mais qui regroupe à peu près tous les cas de figure possibles. On tend actuellement à définir à partir de ces diverses pratiques deux grands systèmes économiques: l'économie de subsistance et l'économie d'échange, en insistant, pour celle-ci, sur les exportations à grande distance. Mais une part importante de la céramique antique, ou en tout cas romaine, ressortit à une catégorie intermédiaire, encore trop peu étudiée, et que caractérisent des échanges intenses, mais 'de proximité': la céramique de Gnathia en est un bon exemple.

3. - Modalités du commerce.

Nous nous sommes jusqu'ici borné à constater – ou à contester – les transports d'objets et de séries, les transferts de modèles et d'ateliers. Il resterait à s'interroger sur les modalités du commerce, lorsque commerce il y a.

3.1. – Je n'aborderai guère que par prétérition les problèmes qui ont plutôt trait à la production: si importants, passionnants et énigmatiques soient-ils, ils ne sont pas au coeur des questions proprement commerciales.

3.1.1. – *Identité et statut des producteurs.* Cette question reste l'une des plus ardues, même quand les céramiques portent des marques – dont nous sommes souvent loin de savoir qui elles désignent. *A fortiori* pour les céramiques rigoureusement anonymes, comme le sont, il faut le remarquer, celles qui ont donné lieu à la plus grande diffusion commerciale, du corinthien ou du bucchero à la céramique attique à vernis noir, de la campanienne A aux sigillées claires.

3.1.2. – *Production rurale et production urbaine.* La tendance récente à insister sur le caractère rural de certaines grandes productions céramiques, comme la sigillée claire, me semble devoir être tempérée. En tout cas, partout où une vérification s'avère possible, le grand commerce apparaît lié à une production *urbaine* au sens strict (Athènes, Naples, Arezzo, Pise, Lyon, etc.).

3.1.3. – *Commerce et 'prospérité'.* Exportation lointaine et soutenue ne signifie pas prospérité des individus ou des communautés qui produisent. Il est possible qu'un artisanat actif et inventif, dont les produits sont consommés sur place, induise plus de prospérité que des productions largement diffusées au loin mais, de ce fait, produites nécessairement au plus juste prix: c'est par exemple un problème qui se pose impérieusement à propos du contraste entre la Grande-Grèce des IVe-IIIe s. et celle des IIe-Ier s. av.n.è.

3.2. – Le transport et la vente.

3.2.1. – *Les modes de transport.* Le transport par eau se taille évidemment la part du lion, et les acquisitions récentes de la céramologie n'ont fait que renforcer cette certitude, en gommant ce qui pouvait apparaître comme des exceptions. Ainsi l'arétine constitue-t-elle beaucoup moins qu'on ne le pensait un cas particulier, dès lors que ses principaux producteurs n'ont eu de cesse de se rapprocher de la mer (Pise), puis de s'établir le long de la voie fluviale Rhône-Saône, essentielle pour les communications avec la Germanie (Lyon). De même est-il de plus en plus clair que la grande production côtière que fut la campanienne A n'a connu en Italie interne qu'une pénétration infime.

3.2.2. – Aquatique ou terrestre, le transport d'un produit aussi sujet à la concurrence et comportant aussi peu de 'valeur ajoutée' que la céramique se conçoit mal si son *coût* n'est pas réduit au minimum possible. La solution la plus évidente consiste à transporter la céramique en surnombre par rapport à des produits (agricoles surtout) plus pondéreux et plus coûteux. Les exemples en ce sens se multiplient à mesure que progressent les fouilles d'épaves et, surtout, l'identification de conteneurs (les amphores) jusqu'alors méconnus ou négligés. D'où une série de diptyques: bucchero et amphores étrusques, céramique corinthienne et amphores corinthiennes, céramique ionienne et amphores ioniennes, campanienne A et amphores Dressel I, sigillée claire et blé ou huile d'Afrique ... Des exceptions réelles ou apparentes nous invitent, soit à combler les lacunes éventuelles de nos connaissances, soit plutôt à nous interroger sur le caractère particulier des systèmes commerciaux qui contredisent cette règle: je pense en particulier à l'exportation de la céramique attique, notamment à vernis noir, ou à celle de la campanienne A avant l'apparition des amphores Dressel I, notamment à Carthage.

3.2.3. – *Les agents du transport.* Deux grands problèmes ici. D'abord, les rapports entre producteurs et négociants: il est probable que les uns se confondent d'autant moins avec les autres que l'ampleur du commerce s'accroît. A l'intérieur de ce premier problème, d'autre part, se pose la question des intermédiaires. Il est certain que dans de nombreux cas des céramiques ont été transportées sur leur lieu de consommation non pas directement, mais moyennant des étapes marquées par des processus de regroupement ou de redistribution. La fameuse caisse trouvée à Pompéi et contenant des vases de La Graufesenque et des lampes d'Italie du Nord suggère comment des grossistes ou demi-grossistes regroupaient et répartissaient les marchandises. Mais le problème des intermédiaires offre un autre aspect, surtout autour de la Méditerranée morcelée de la haute époque: la redistribution dans un pays A, par une ethnie B, des produits d'une autre ethnie C, préalablement importés en B et mêlés, minoritairement, aux produits exportés par B. Pensons par exemple aux céramiques grecques du VIIe s. en Gaule par rapport aux céramiques étrusques, ou aux céramiques grecques des IVe-IIIe s. redistribuées par Carthage dans le monde punique. Sans compter le rôle, souvent oublié, que durent nécessairement jouer les 'indigènes' dans ces processus. Autant de cas, en somme, où il serait imprudent de conclure sans autre forme de procès à un commerce direct entre les deux extrémités de la chaîne.

3.3. – Clientèles et consommation.

3.3.1. – *Les prix et les modalités de l'achat* sont un des secteurs les plus mal connus du sujet qui nous intéresse ici, et nous ne devons guère compter sur les sources littéraires ou épigraphiques, en nombre dérisoire et qui concernent exclusivement l'époque impériale. On a supposé que la sigillée se vendait bien auprès d'une clientèle militaire qui pouvait payer en espèces. Soit: mais comment devons-nous imaginer le commerce à des distances considérables, puis la vente, de produits aussi infimes que les vases ordinaires, en dehors des circuits monétaires? Comment les 'consommateurs' de la Gaule, de l'Ibérie, de l'Afrique se procuraient-ils un canthare étrusque, une coupe ionienne, une patère attique, un bol en campanienne A? Le troc, bien sûr. Mais ce mot commode recouvre en réalité une ignorance profonde des mécanismes par lesquels des objets de peu de valeur pouvaient parvenir dans les modestes cases d'un oppidum perdu, avec une abondance que nous avons peine à imaginer (pour la campanienne A, probablement plusieurs vases par habitant).

3.3.2. – Des *termes de l'échange*, la céramique est à peu près le seul à être parvenu jusqu'à nous, et ce n'est pas le moindre de ses intérêts que d'être ainsi le révélateur de trafics dont elle ne représente en soi qu'un aspect souvent mineur. Le bucchero et surtout les amphores étrusques, la campanienne et surtout les amphores italiques, nous suggèrent ainsi que l'Etrurie, que Rome, cherchaient en Gaule des fournitures – esclaves, produits de l'agriculture, de l'élevage et des mines – qui n'ont laissé aucune trace dans le sol, et fort peu dans les textes. C'est donc l'étude de la distribution géographique, chronologique, quantitative de la céramique qui nous orientera vers les solutions les plus vraisemblables; et nous nous apercevrons, alors, qu'elle est spécialement dense, entre autres, dans certaines régions minières.

3.3.3. – *Qui sont les clients* du commerce à grande distance? Pour l'époque impériale, on a souligné le poids de la clientèle militaire dans la consommation de la sigillée (d'où le déplacement vers le *limes* de la production d''arétine') ou des lampes de terre cuite. Mais à l'époque archaïque ou républicaine ce sont des communautés qui n'ont rien de spécialement militaire qui absorbent, par exemple, l'essentiel des exportations de campanienne: nouveau motif de réflexion sur la différence de nature entre le commerce des premiers siècles de l'Empire et celui de la longue période qui les a précédés.

3.3.4. – Les clients exercent-ils quelque *influence* sur le commerce de la céramique? Arrive-t-il que la demande oriente l'offre? Certainement, et cela non seulement pour les vases-conteneurs, mais aussi pour les vases-marchandises. Des traditions locales, des habitudes de table ou de cuisine, des goûts divers selon les ethnies modèlent le faciès des céramiques reçues, acceptées, dans chaque contrée. Ce phénomène d'influence de l'aval vers l'amont est encore mal étudié et l'érudition moderne, volontiers axée sur l'économique pur, n'envisage qu'avec réticence les problèmes de goût. Ce genre d'explication permet pourtant de tempérer, de nuancer les hypothèses 'catastrophistes' qui tendraient à voir dans chaque interruption ou ralentissement d'importations d'un type céramique, dans chaque différence de faciès entre deux sites, le résultat d'un blocus, d'une décadence ou d'un conflit politique. Il doit être considéré aussi dans l'étude des circuits commerciaux ou des 'appropriations de marchés', car la réussite d'une production tient entre autres à son adaptation aux goûts d'une clientèle potentielle.

4. – On a observé qu'il était possible d'écrire l'histoire *de* la céramique, mais non l'histoire *par* la céramique. Si secondaire qu'ait été la céramique dans la réalité antique, ce jugement est excessif, dès lors qu'on utilise les indices céramiques de façon prudente, ample, comparative, notamment en surveillant les différences et les variations à l'intérieur d'un système géographique ou chronologique donné.

Ainsi, lorsque nous considérons les céramiques à vernis noir d'Occident, nous constatons une mosaïque incroyablement bigarrée de petites productions, quelques productions modérément exportées, et un géant (la campanienne A). Si nous considérons d'autre part les exportations céramiques depuis l'Italie, toutes catégories et toutes périodes confondues, nous constatons qu'il est peu d'époques où elles soient notables: il s'agit de l'époque archaïque (bucchero) et, à un degré infiniment supérieur, des IIe-Ier s. (campanienne A), le cas de l'arétine apparaissant désormais, on l'a vu, comme différent.

Si enfin nous regroupons ces deux tableaux, nous constatons combien est exceptionnel ce qui se passe en termes de céramique dans l'Italie centrale tyrrhénienne aux deux derniers siècles de la République: ce sont la seule époque, la seule région dont la production céramique ait été orientée aussi majoritairement, aussi massivement vers la standardisation et vers l'exportation à partir d'un seul atelier. Dussions-nous n'en avoir aucun autre indice, cela suffirait probablement à nous garantir qu'un nouvel ordre économique s'est développé alors dans cette région, celui-là même qui suscite actuellement tant d'attention sous le nom de système de production esclavagiste. Et c'est encore la céramique qui constitue un des indices les plus nets de la rupture qui intervient après la seconde guerre punique entre 'arte popolare' et 'arte colta', et que traduit aussi, à la même époque, l'âpreté des débats autour de la notion de *luxuria*.

La céramique fait ici partie d'un faisceau de données dont aucune n'est par nature inférieure aux autres. Il en est de même, par exemple, pour les lignes de fracture économiques et culturelles qui se dessinent au IIe s. de n.è. dans le monde romain, et par lesquelles, notamment, l'Italie se sépare de l'Europe pour se souder à l'Afrique – c'est-à-dire, en termes de céramique, passe des sigillées 'européennes' à la sigillée claire.

Oui, l'histoire, et pas seulement l'histoire économique, ne peut aisément se passer des témoignages de la céramique – témoignages 'involontaires' et par là même particulièrement significatifs: mais à la condition expresse que nous procédions par des dénombrements au moins approximatifs, par des identifications exactes et précises, et en comparant ce qui est comparable. Car faute de ces précautions, on peut faire dire à la céramique ce que l'on veut, et l'histoire a autant à y perdre que la céramologie.

Aix-en-Provence   JEAN-PAUL MOREL

9. THE ROMAN ARMY AND LONG DISTANCE TRADE*

The Roman army was not only the tool which created the empire, it was also an important agent in transmitting the Roman way of life to the provinces. This took place not simply by example, through building programmes, veteran colonies and so on, but also by the creation of networks of contact which resulted in the interplay of Roman and Native groups.[1] The extent of Romanisation in a province is in part a direct reflection of the success with which such structures became established and their stability over time.

One of the indices often used as a measure of Romanisation is the material assemblage of 'imported' fine ware pottery and wine amphorae. This is usually taken to be the result of civilian long-distance trade and is seen as representing a potential body of ideas which flowed along the trade routes. A significant new contribution to this school of thought has been presented by André Tchernia in a recent paper on the importation of Italian wines into Gaul.[2] What Tchernia has established beyond any reasonable doubt is that substantial quantities of wine were exchanged for metals and/or slaves during the last century of the Republic, a trade that was curtailed when Augustus initiated the reorganisation of the Gallic provinces.

The questions, however, which must be posed side by side with Tchernia's important paper are: (a) whether there has not been a serious underestimation of the military traffic during the second and first centuries B.C., to the point where the civilian trade has overshadowed the whole transaction; and (b) to what extent the civilian trade could have grown up independent of military supplies and consumption – even if, in the end, it assumed its own dynamic as long as the specialised demand for Gallic slaves in Italy remained high.

As to the first question, concerning the military demand for wine, Tchernia has minimized it on two counts which I find unconvincing. First, he suggests that Roman troops were not accustomed to drinking wine as part of their standard rations, and that they drank 'vinegar' instead – *acetum*. (In fact Davies translates *acetum* as 'sour wine', which it almost certainly was.)[3] But our literary evidence shows that ordinary wine was part of the soldiers' daily diet. Appian, for instance, writing of the Spanish wars in the mid second century B.C. records the *unusual* circumstances which deprived troops of both wine (*oinos*) and *acetum* (*oxos*) (App. *Iber.* 54). The elder Pliny, who was exceedingly pedantic in matters of terminology (note, for instance, his insistence that the word for wine in Cato the Elder's day was not *vinum* but *temetum*), says that the humble rowers in the Roman fleet during Cato's Spanish campaigns in the second century B.C. drank *vinum* – of poor quality, to be sure, but not *acetum* (Pliny, *nat. hist.* 14.91 – (Cato) *non aliud vinum bibit quam remiges*). As it happens, both Appian and Pliny were experts on military matters in their own day.

An army of four legions in Gaul was far from unusual in the last century of the Republic.[4] Pompey's army was a good deal larger than this, and Caesar began with an army of that size. During the civil war there were as many as eleven legions at one time present in Gaul. And this says nothing about troops in Spain (who would receive their supplies along the Gallic coast) or about auxiliaries (cf. Caes. *Bell. Gall.* 7.34 – Aedui). Four legions means the presence of at least 20,000 men who, if they drank the litre of wine per day that today's Frenchman drinks, would have consumed at least seven million litres (70,000 hectolitres) per year. This is as much as the total traffic of 50,000 hectolitres per year calculated by Tchernia on the basis of the evidence from shipwrecks. My intention is not to argue away the considerable Italian wine trade among the Celts, but to suggest that the military traffic must always have been a significant, probably the major part of the goods moving along the Gallic coast.

About the second question, that is, the independence of civilian trade, I shall have more to say in a general way later on. Undoubtedly civilian trade did sometimes precede the flag, as Caesar found when he arrived in Gaul (Caes. *Bell. Gall.* 4.2). But it is impossible to ignore the fact that the great boom in the export of Dressel I A and B wine amphorae, which characterised Italian trade to Gaul from the last quarter of the second century B.C. to the last decade of the first century B.C., coincides almost precisely with the main Roman military effort in Gaul between the period of the marking out of the military road from Ampurias to the Rhône c. 150 B.C. and the campaigns of Julius Caesar and Augustus (up to Drusus's Rhine offensive).

Tchernia uses, as one of his arguments for civilian trade, the contrast between the widespread distribution of Dressel I amphorae all over France and Britain, often found in huge dumps, and the relatively limited distribution of Dressel 20 amphorae which were containers for the export of Spanish olive oil from the time of Augustus and are mainly found in quite small quantities along the military supply routes of the Rhône-Rhine axis. How fair a comparison this is must be a matter for dispute. We do not, after all, have very much information about the location of the armies of Caesar or Augustus in Gaul;[5] so it is not easy to distinguish military supply routes from purely civilian routes in the first century B.C.; nor to compare them with military supply routes of a different epoch. Wine amphorae were also treated differently from oil amphorae, since (as Tchernia notes) the wine was almost certainly transferred from the amphorae into barrels at specified inland supply points, leaving behind the huge caches of pottery which have brought the dumps to the notice of archaeologists. Oil jars, as far as one can see, were not treated like this and so became much more scattered.

One of the examples used by Tchernia to corroborate his case for civilian consumption of wine in Gaul is drawn from the famous passage in Cicero's speech *Pro Fonteio*, defending a Roman governor, Marcus Fonteius, against the *crimen vinarium* with which he was charged. Although the subject has received a considerable amount of attention over the last twenty years,[6] a fact to be explained by the boom in archaeological evidence which can be used to amplify and clarify the written sources for the trade in Italian wines to south-west Gaul, I propose to review it again to demonstrate the intimate connection between military supply routes and civilian long-distance trade. After which I shall test the conclusions against the evidence from imperial Gaul.

Despite the scholarly activity, the nature and purpose of the scheme devised by Fonteius, and the conclusions that may be drawn regarding the wine trade between Italy and Gaul are by no means clear. The text of the charge is as follows:

> *Cognoscite nunc de crimine uinario, quod illi inuidiosissimum et maximum esse uoluerunt. Crimen a Plaetorio, iudices, ita constitutum est, M. Fonteio non in Gallia primum uenisse in mentem ut portorium uini institueret, sed hac inita iam ac proposita ratione Roma profectum. Itaque Titurium Tolosae quaternos denarios in singulas uini amphoras portori nomine exegisse; Croduni Porcium et Munium ternos <et> uictoriatum, Vulchalone Seruaeum binos et uictoriatum; atque in his locis (sc. Croduni et Vulchalone) ab iis portorium esse exactum, si qui Cobiomago, qui uicus inter Tolosam et Narbonem est, deuerterentur neque Tolosa ire uellent; Elesiodunis C. Annium senos denarios ab iis qui ad hostem portarent exegisse. Video, iudices, esse crimen et genere ipso magnum – uectigal enim esse impositum fructibus nostris dicitur, et pecuniam permagnam ratione ista cogi potuisse confiteor – et inuidiam uel <maximam>; maxime enim inimici hanc rem sermonibus diuolgare uoluerunt.*

> *pro Font.* 9.19-20

The central points of the charge as Cicero gives them, then, are:

(i)   that a scheme was hatched before Fonteius ever set out for his province.

(ii)   by this scheme wine in transit from *Narbo* (Narbonne) was to be taxed at a rate that varied according to its destination. Thus:

    (*a*)   at Tolosa (Toulouse) a duty of 4 *den*/amphora

    (*b*)   at Crodunum (?) 3½ *den*/amphora

    (*c*)   at Vulchalo (?) 2½ *den*/amphora

    (*d*)   *in his locis* (sc. Crodunum et Vulchalo) an unspecified levy was to be exacted on wine turning away from the main road at Cobiomagus (?)

    (*e*)   at Elesiodunum (Montferrand), on wine destined *ad hostem* (perhaps for the Ruteni[7]) a levy of 6 *den*/amphora was imposed.

The location of these toll posts poses major problems, since only Elesiodunum, apart, of course, from Tolosa, can be located with certainty. Existing interpretations of the *crimen vinarium* start from the assumption that Tolosa was privileged under the scheme of Fonteius, and go through various convolutions to establish this fact. It is argued that the origin of the charges must rest either with the Allobroges, angered by the diversion of wine to western Transalpina which would otherwise have been marketed amongst their own people, or with the Italian wine producer who found their trade reduced by a rise in prices occasioned by the additional levy. Or, as most recent views favour (including that of Tchernia), the case was prompted by those Gauls who were forced to pay more for their wine as a result of a corrupt tax.

None of these interpretations is totally satisfactory. There is no evidence for a radical shift of Italian wine exports from the Rhone Valley to western Transalpina. Indeed the conclusion of a study on the stamped amphorae of Sestius suggests quite the contrary trend.[8] The view that the consumers' response to a rise in prices was a fall in demand, is too modern a notion to be assumed, especially when we consider the social context of native wine consumption in southern Gaul.[9] Moreover, if Italians had been the originators of the charge against Fonteius then it is inconceivable that Cicero could have made such play of the un-Roman nature of the prosecution's case.[10]

Although the levy could only have applied to wine for civilian consumption there is no reason in the literary evidence for supposing that most of the wine was intended for markets outside the province. In making this assumption, Etienne sought to provide some literary underpinning to the archaeological evidence for a trade in wine from Narbo to Burdigala (Bordeaux).[11] But why should Cicero specify the single levy at Elesiodunum as for wine traded *ad hostem* unless it were uniquely so? Indeed, a distribution map of amphorae of the period discovered in South-West Gaul shows clearly that the major discoveries have been within the province, at Tolosa in particular.

Elesiodunum was the toll point for wine destined *ad hostem*, and was carried at the highest attested rate of 6 *den*/amphora. For these reasons, it was set apart by Cicero. Cobiomagus was mentioned alone, as evidently it did not possess a toll post of its own, although a special rate of duty was registered for traffic passing through that settlement. The first three locations, Tolosa, Crodunum and Vulchalo, like Elesiodunum, required no further explanation as to their location (unlike Cobiomagus, which is given a gloss). This was for the reason, I suggest, that they were all garrison posts, known to Cicero's audience.

The existence of a Roman garrison at Tolosa is attested in 106 B.C., and the quasi-military character of Narbo was still relevant at the time of the trial.[12] In the circumstances of Fonteius' governship (the continuing Sertorian war in Spain, unrest amongst the tribes of Transalpina), we can be sure that other garrisons existed, especially on the road linking Narbo and Tolosa, and that one of these was likely to have been at Carcaso, which one commentator has noted as the possible identity of Vulchalo.[13] If Cicero first enumerated garrison towns, we could identify

Crodunum with Sostomagus (Castelnaudary) on the grounds of it too being a likely garrison site. Cobiomagus would thus control the route southwards to join the protohistoric trackway across the ridges of southern Lauragais, an area of large amphora finds for the period with which we are concerned.

Fonteius' scheme, then, was probably based upon the garrison posts along the strategic route from Narbo to Tolosa. Elesiodunum, specifically dealing with extra-provincial trade, was liable to the heaviest tax, but the other posts were levied accorded to a sliding duty, weighted with distance from Narbo, the port.

Thus Tolosa, far from being the most privileged centre, emerges as the hardest hit of the provincial communities named. This loyal community was therefore being penalised by the wine levy just as though it had been a barbarian settlement outside the province, whilst its status as an ally of the Roman people should have afforded it protection from such treatment. Cicero's insulting remarks about Gallic drinking habits were calculated to obscure this important fact.[14] We can see the full context of the *crimen* and its implications more clearly if we look briefly at the military situation in Transalpina during the 70s B.C.

The war against Sertorius and the remnants of the Marian supporters in Spain was conducted throughout the 70s, using Transalpina as the army's base and supply line. The fighting was initially prosecuted by Metellus, and then in 77-76 Pompeius marched westwards through Transalpina to continue the war effort. In the context of the war, western Transalpina assumed major significance: Metellus wintered his army there in 75-74 and Pompeius did likewise in the winters of 77-76 and 74-73. This was the background to the programme of road construction and vigorous requisitioning of cavalry, corn and money by Fonteius. It is known that the confiscations carried out by the same governor were to implement decisions made by Pompeius in response to opposition he had encountered on his march to Spain. This latter task involved Fonteius in some active campaigning.[15]

In addition to the burdens of confiscations and war requisitioning over a succession of years for an army of unusually large size, Transalpina also suffered at this time from a grain shortage.[16] We may well imagine that problems of supply were a continual concern for Fonteius, and Cicero emphasised his services in this field on behalf of the Roman People.[17]

Since Fonteius was directly concerned with the major task of organising essential supplies for the troops under his command, it makes sense that one element of those supplies would have been wine, shipped from Italy. As Tchernia has noted, analysis of the contents of shipwrecks along the south Gallic coast reveals that over fifty per cent can be assigned to the last two centuries of the Republican period, when troops were stationed in south-west Transalpina.[18] By contrast, only fifteen per cent date from the first two centuries after Christ, at which time the focus of military activity was centred on the Rhineland.

Given the necessity of supplying the troops with such commodities on a regular basis, there would have been ample opportunity for private sales to 'ride on the back' of official cargoes. It is in this context that the *crimen vinarium* makes best sense, namely as an attempt by Fonteius to extract additional taxes from the secondary trade which had already passed through the garrison posts on the military road, because it had come in the same cargoes as the military supplies themselves. The complaint, therefore, must have arisen from civilian consumers who were forced to pay further indirect levies on top of the harsh direct burdens already imposed upon them for the maintenance of the military garrisons in the province.

The relationship between army supply and long distance trade is clearly seen in this episode: the requirements of the army for bulk supplies transported over long distance (in this instance wine from Italy) created a traffic onto which could be attached a civilian trade, the extent of which has for the first time been brought out by Tchernia. This trade however was immaterial to the military administration which, under an unscrupulous Governor, was prepared to exploit it to the full. When the direction of army supply routes changed in the early empire in response to new troop dispositions, then the civilian long-distance trade collapsed and was forced to pursue the new opportunities presented by the reorientated official supply line.[19]

We can trace this change by looking at another example of a trade-good, *terra sigillata* (TS). The earliest Gallic kilns known to have produced TS date from the Augustian period.[20] The earlier Campanian and Arretine wares which were shipped to Gaul mirror the change we have discussed in relation to amphorae, and it is significant that Lugdunum, a key point in the supply system for Augustus' northerly troop advances, was chosen by the earliest TS potters based in Gaul. Although there is some doubt about the destination of the earliest potters' products, a second group of potters working at la Muette on the left bank of the Saône distributed their vessels predominantly in the military zone. The concentration of military activity north of Lugudum was, then, the chief stimulus in the establishment of TS manufacture in this area.

It has long been accepted, of course, that the military 'market' was attractive to traders, and indeed the emergence of a number of centres of TS manufacture in eastern Gaul during the later first century is rightly seen as a response to the opportunities for trade presented by the military zone. What is not clear, however, is the extent to which the pottery trade was able to exploit the market through its own initiative, rather than depend upon the pre-existence of other factors. The intimate connection between the growth of a major civilian trade and army supply routes suggested by the *crimen vinarium* suggests that there was no truly independent dynamic of trade. This can be further substantiated by examples from the TS industry.

I have argued elsewhere that the success of la Graufesenque as a TS centre lay in its ability to exploit an official transport link between silver mines on the southern slopes of the Causses and the coast. The withdrawal of this transport link coincided with the breakdown of long distance trading in la Graufesenque TS.[21] A similar dependence upon official supply lines is implied by evidence from eastern Gaul. The late first century TS potters at Boucheporn (Moselle) distributed their product northwards to Mogontiacum and the lower Rhine valley, and eastwards to Argentorate and the Agri Decumates.[22] Two routes are implied here, the first by river, the second overland. During the second century, the potters moved their workshops further to the east, nearer to the military road linking Divodurum (Metz) and Argentorate. This evident preference for a land route with all its disadvantages when compared to a water outlet was not dictated by clay resources and implies that the primary interest of the potters lay in the road link to the Rhine rift valley. It is significant not only that Argentorate was a legionary base with the militarised Agri Decumates beyond, but also that the road in question was a vital supply line for those garrisons, probably providing grain and iron from Lorraine, as was emphasised in the later empire when the road was defended by a series of fortified posts.[23]

Epigraphic evidence enables us to go further in establishing the fundamental link between army requirements and long distance trade. The incidence of Gallic inscriptions which record traders (*negotiatores*) in goods like wine and pottery enable us to compare the relative significance of military and civilian markets. Of thirteen pottery traders, eight have been found within the Rhineland military zone and two more barely beyond it, at Trier and Metz. The exceptions, from Lyon, significantly include one trader who was a veteran from legio I Minerva, stationed in Lower Germany.[24] A similar picture is revealed by wine traders' inscriptions, although the greater significance of Lyon points to the obvious fact that much of the wine consumed on the Rhine was drawn from the Mediterranean zone.

One further example of the principle that long distance trade depended upon official supply lines for its existence can be adduced from the marginal trade in grain which is attested in the epigraphic evidence. Grain, because of its bulk and general availability, was only rarely shipped over long distance. The establishment of the Rhine frontier with its large permanent garrisons, however, made demands for grain which went far beyond the potential of the frontier zone itself. Large areas of northern Gaul were geared towards the production of a grain surplus for the Rhineland, and other areas were regularly called upon to supplement these basic supplies. It was this regular and necessary bulk shipment of staples over long distance which created the transport facility exploited by individual entrepreneurs. All the small scale traders of Gaul can be explained in these terms, living a parasitic existence on the back of a massive official supply system. Four grain traders are known, one from Lugdunum, the other three all firmly within the military zone.[25] It is worth emphasising that, as with wine and pottery traders, this kind of entrepreneurial activity is only attested in close association with the military garrisons.

The evidence from Gaul is unanimous therefore in the picture it paints of the relationship between the Roman army and long distance trade. Of necessity the army garrisons drew bulked supplies from regions far beyond their *territoria*. The regular transport system which was created to transfer those vital goods to the frontiers provided an opportunity of assured transport to a stable and attractive market, the soldiers. Inevitably some entrepreneurs were able and willing to capitalise on such an opportunity. And, as Tchernia has argued, this opportunity on certain favourable occasions, such as a high demand for slaves, could become a trade of sizeable proportions. All this, however, was a spin off of no direct concern to the administration. In no real sense was it vital to the soldiers, nor was it central, I submit, to the subsistence of the huge majority of producers in the economy.[26] Long distance trade, therefore, cannot be regarded as having contributed significantly either to the economy of the provinces or to their feeling of identity with the empire. Rather it was itself a manifestation of the paramount contribution of the Roman army in these areas.

Peterborough   PAUL MIDDLETON

NOTES

1. By example: Tac. *Ann.* 12.32 (*Colonia Victricensis* at Camulodunum); *Agric.* 21 (encouragement to adopt habits and customs under military government stimulus).
   Networks of contact: for example, the role of troops in everyday police work; the organisation involved in supplying the army with basic necessities; the generation of services around the military camps in response to the spending power of the troops.

2. A. Tchernia, 'Italian wine trade in Gaul at the end of the Republic' in P. Garnsey, K. Hopkins and C. R. Whittaker (edd.), *Trade in the ancient economy* (1983) 87-104.

3. Davies, *Britannia* 2 (1971) 124, cited by Tchernia; cf. *Thes. Ling. Lat.* 1.379, s.v. 'acetum'.

4. See the table in P. A. Brunt, *Italian Manpower* (1971) 44; in Spain in the 70s there were as many as fourteen legions.

5. For a recent attempt to show the widespread distribution of troops in early Gaul, see E. M. Wightman, 'Military arrangements, native settlements and related developments in early Roman Gaul', *Helinium* 17 (1977) 105-26.

6. Cicero, *pro Fonteio*. The most influential scholars to have discussed the matter are R. Etienne, *Bordeaux Antique* (1960) 90-100, M. Labrousse, *Toulouse Antique* (1968) 137-60, G. Clemente, *I Romani nella Gallia meridionale* (1974) 130-6.

7. This is a guess, but seems the only plausible interpretation; cf. Etienne (1960) 95, n. 98; Labrousse (1968) 142, n. 34.

8. Y. Roman, 'La place du couloir Rhodanien dans la diffusion des amphores de Sestius', *REA* 25 (1974) 133-4.

9. That is, ostentatious aristocratic display of hospitality; cf. Diod. Sic. 5.26.3-4 on the value placed on wine by the native aristocracies. This is well brought out by Tchernia (n. 2) 94.

10. See, for example, *pro Font.* 3.4 *lubidinis barbarorum*.

11. Etienne (n. 6) 96; Labrousse (n. 6) 142.

12. Garrison at Tolosa: Dio 27.90; a possible fortlet has been located at Vieille-Toulouse, G. Fouet, 'Le grand axe commercial Toulousain sous la règne d'Auguste', *Caesarodunum* 12 (1977) 470, n. 19. Narbo's role: *pro Font.* 5.13.

13. Mgr. Griffe, 'La Narbonnaise occidentale au temps du preteur Fonteius', *AM* 69 (1957) 63.

14. E. Badian, 'Notes on provincia Gallia in the late Republic', R. Chevallier (*ed.*), *Mélanges A. Piganiol* 2 (1966) 912, notes that Tolosa had no special privileges at this time.

15. Fonteius' activity included road building (*pro Font.* 8.17-18), requisitions and confiscations (6.13), and campaigning (5.12).

16. Sallust, *Epist. Cn. Pompei* 9; see note 4 for the huge legionary army in Spain, to which Brunt adds another four legions for the Gauls.

17. *pro Font.* 5.12, 6.13.

18. R. Lequemont, B. Liou, 'Les épaves de la côte de Transalpine', *Cahiers Ligures* 24 (1975) 76-82.

19. Cf. Roman (n. 8).

20. J. Lasfargues, 'Une industrie Lyonnaise', *Archeologia* 50 (1972) 15-9.

21. P. Middleton, 'La Graufesenque: a question of marketing', *Athenaeum* 58 (1980) 186-91.

22. M. Lutz, *La sigillée de Boucheporn* (1977) 172, fig. 60.

23. Defended road: cf. H. Schönberger, 'The Roman frontier in Germany', *JRS* 59 (1969) 144-97.

24. *CIL* XIII 1906 (Lyon); cf. P. Middleton, 'Army supply in Roman Gaul: an hypothesis for Roman Britain', B. C. Burnham, H. B. Johnson (*edd.*) *Invasion and Response* (1979) 85.

25. *CIL* XIII 1972 (Lyon); 7068 (Mainz); 7836 (Aachen); 8725 (Nijmegen).

26. In this discussion, I have implicitly rejected the notion that army supplies themselves constituted a trade. On this much larger question, and the implications of this view see my detailed arguments, sketched in Middleton (n. 24) 87-90, in *Trade and market in Roman Imperial Gaul* (B.A.R. forthcoming).

* I am grateful to Michael Crawford, Peter Garnsey and Dick Whittaker for their helpful comments on an earlier draft of my thoughts on the *Crimen vinarium*.

10. MODELS, SHIPS AND STAPLES

This paper falls into two halves. In the first part, I construct a rough model, in order to show up some probable relationships within the Roman economy, for example, between country and town, trade and taxation, entrepôts and major markets. The main objective is to understand the implications for the Roman economy of staples (wheat, barley, wine, olive oil), transported by farmers usually for sale to, and for consumption by, the inhabitants of towns. In the second part, I concentrate on two issues of detail, the cost of Roman ships and the costs of transport. I argue that Romans commonly used ships of over 350 tonnes burden on the empire's main shipping routes, and that the cost of these large ships was so high that members of the Roman elite were probably involved in their construction and use. I also argue that the surviving Roman testimony on transport prices is untrustworthy. In any case, the importance of transport costs has been overemphasised in estimates of the volume of trade over land and sea in the Roman world.

I. *A Rough Model*

Modern orthodoxy about the ancient economy holds that inter-regional trade was low in volume, because such trade was primarily concerned with luxuries for a small, wealthy elite; it is argued that staples were seldom moved long distances in bulk, except as taxes in kind, partly because of the high cost of transport especially overland, and partly because of the low purchasing power of most consumers, who lived near the level of minimum subsistence; and finally, that traders, even those involved in luxuries, were typically men of small means. Let me stress that this is not, nor is it intended as, a complete description of current orthodoxy.[1] But it is sufficient for my present purposes, because it highlights certain aspects over which I should like to take issue.

I have argued elsewhere that the scale of inter-regional trade in staples and in crafted goods (textiles, leather, pots) was considerable, because of the distance between where money taxes were typically levied and where they were spent. I have also argued that the Finley-Jones model of the ancient economy needs to be modified to accommodate modest but significant economic growth in the Mediterranean basin in ancient times, peaking in the first two centuries A.D. I have also argued that by no means all peasants lived at the level of minimum subsistence. Their aggregate demand, for cloth, tools and occasional purchases of minor luxuries, constituted a major dynamic element in Roman trade.[2]

These arguments taken together imply a greater volume of trade than is usually assumed within the dominant orthodoxy. For the sake of convenience, I shall divide trade into three categories: long-distance, that is inter-regional trade; medium-range, intra-regional, inter-town trade; and short haul, local trade between the countryside and a nearby market town. The term region is unavoidably vague; I am thinking of large areas such as Egypt or Syria or southern Gaul. I should stress that these three types of trade interlocked. The exaction of money taxes and their expenditure predominantly in the city of Rome or in frontier provinces stimulated long-distance, inter-regional trade. To put it crudely, tax-payers had to sell goods in those distant parts in order to earn money with which to pay the next year's taxes. Not that this exchange was a simple, two-way process between tax-payers on the one hand and tax-spenders (soldiers and courtiers) on the other. The interchange worked through a complex network of trade, in which towns were the intermediate nodes. Local trade fed into medium-range and inter-regional trade and *vice versa*.

The complexities of the network can best be envisaged by considering the fate of the surplus. Prosperous peasants consumed some of the food surplus themselves.[3] All the rest of the surplus was either (a) transported to a nearby market to be sold, or was delivered in kind (b) as tax, or (c) as rent to landlords. Most food, it should be stressed, was consumed on the farm where it was produced. Of the surplus, most was carted or shipped only a short distance. This short-haul transport of the agricultural surplus, typically by farmers themselves to a nearby market town, constituted the greatest proportion of all transport which occurred in the Roman world.[4]

Given the absence of any explicit testimony, it must seem hopeless to estimate the volume of food transported short-haul in the Roman empire. But a first fix can be simply made. If the proportion of the empire's total population (>50 million people) living in towns and in urban occupations (*i.e.* not growing their own food) was 10-15%, and if they lived at the level of minimum subsistence (*c.* 220kg wheat equivalent per person/year), then the volume of food was at least 1.1-1.7 million tonnes each year.[5] To this we must add fuel, clothing and building materials. In so far as urban dwellers lived above the minimum level of subsistence and consumed other goods imported from towns (metals, artefacts), then the volume of short-haul transport was even greater. Without any commitment as to its truth, let us tentatively estimate short-haul transport of food from farms to towns in the Roman empire in the first two centuries as at least 1,500,000 tonnes each year. (Table 2: A + B + C). I should stress that this is a low estimate, based on the consumption of food alone in towns at the level of minimum subsistence. Even so, we can then use this estimate as a bench-mark for the judgement of other figures.

Our next problem is (a) to trace the surplus as it was distributed to consumers and (b) to estimate the volume which was consumed locally or transported further. I shall deal first with food sent on as tax in kind, then with rent in kind, with food sold in the local market and transhipped unconverted to Rome, to other very large cities, and to smaller market towns; and finally, I shall deal with the surplus consumed locally in the peasants' nearby market town. My tentative estimates of quantities are set out in Table 2. Such figures may drive the sober ancient historian to rage, derision or drink. But they are meant to be helpful in two ways. First, these estimates give rough orders of magnitude to dimensions which would otherwise remain nebulous – 'huge' 'very large' 'a small proportion'. Secondly, these figures help establish probabilities and relationships. That has been my own experience in writing this paper. I have been forced to realise, in a way that I had never done before, the huge volume and value of food and goods sold and moved in Roman commerce outside the immediate district of production and the considerable sums of capital involved. The sums were so large that I am now convinced that the upper echelons of Roman society were involved in trade, or that there were very rich merchants outside the elite. But more of that later.

Taxes in Kind

Taxes in kind were delivered primarily in wheat.[6] The biggest target population supported by taxes in kind were citizens living in the city of Rome. They received a free monthly ration of 33kg wheat, more than enough to feed an adult male, but not enough to feed a whole family. Two hundred thousand adult male recipients would have received 80,000 tonnes of wheat per year.[7] I assume that all the wheat and other foods which they and the other inhabitants of Rome (both free and slave) consumed over and above the free wheat distributed by the state, was bought on the open market.

There is considerable doubt as to whether any other segment of the empire's population was fed directly on taxes raised in kind. The Roman government continued to assess taxes in kind (Hyginus 205L), but we do not know whether these taxes in kind were in fact leased out to private tax-farmers, and commuted to money, or exacted as taxes in kind and distributed as such by officials. We do not even know whether Roman soldiers in the first two centuries A.D. were fed primarily on wheat supplied as tax in kind, or if the Roman authorities bought food for soldiers at fixed prices, or on the open market. But we do know that Roman soldiers, legionaries and auxiliaries, were charged for rations (*P. Gen. Lat.* 1 and 4).[8] And it seems a bit odd if soldiers were fed out of wheat tax, but charged cash for their rations. I think that provisioning soldiers with food, raised as tax (*annona*), first became established from the third century A.D. Yet even if we boldly assume that all 300,000 Roman soldiers (legionaries and auxiliaries) were provided with wheat, raised as tax in kind, much earlier and on the same generous scale as given to citizens living in the city of Rome, then their total consumption was 120,000 tonnes per year. Two points can be quickly made. First, taxes in kind raised and distributed as such to sizeable target populations in the first two centuries A.D.

totalled a maximum of 200,000 tonnes of wheat (80,000 tonnes to Rome plus 120,000 tonnes to soldiers); this was a small proportion of the total agricultural surplus transported short-haul (low estimate: 1,500,000 tonnes wheat equivalent). There was no other large population supported by taxes in kind. Secondly, if soldiers were fed out of tax in kind, much of their wheat was supplied locally from land around the garrisons. They were supplied short-haul.

Rents in Kind

The testimony is fragmentary. Most of it comes from Egypt. A very few interesting snippets survive from Italy, but date from the fourth to sixth centuries A.D., when the Roman economy was probably less monetised. In Roman Egypt, in the second and third centuries A.D., according to one substantial survey of the surviving evidence, approximately half the agricultural tenancies were levied in kind, a third were a mixture of money and kind; less than a fifth were exacted in money. From the fourth century A.D., three quarters of the rents were fixed solely in kind; only one sixth were solely in money.[9] Most of the rents were paid in wheat, but barley, lentils and flax also occurred. The type of rent depended mostly on the crop sown. Most rents in kind were on small holdings and were for local consumption by local landlords living in nearby villages and towns.

Larger landowners exacted most of their rents in money. This can be illustrated but not proved with a few known examples (e.g. *P. Goodspeed* 30); and it can be argued theoretically. Large absentee landowners wanted some income in kind: staples for their households, chickens, eggs, ducks, honey, wine and other delicacies for their own table (*P. Ital.* 3). But they needed most of their rental income in cash, in order to buy services (slaves, water) and non-farm goods (houses, fuel, clothes, silks, luxuries). Olympiodorus writing in *c.* A.D. 400 about the central Roman aristocracy, claimed that three quarters of their income was in gold and one quarter was in kind (frag. 44). In the first two centuries A.D., I suspect that the proportion paid in kind was even lower. The record of papal estates (*Liber Pontificalis*) lists private estates given to the church at Rome in the early fourth century; it shows that income from almost all estates was paid exclusively in money.[10] The exceptions are interesting. Some church estates in Egypt were required to deliver considerable quantities of cinnamon, pepper, cloves and nard oil. None of these grow in Egypt. They were imported from India and the East Indies. It seems likely therefore that these estates were forced to buy these precious spices in the open market and send them on to Rome. What happened to them there? It seems likely that they were sold in Rome to yield money for the Church, because they were neither useful for liturgical purposes nor were the clergy numerous enough then to consume such quantities of spices. These rents in kind were closely akin to money rents. In sum, rents in kind were probably only a minor element in long-distance, inter-regional transport, though they may have constituted a significant part of the surplus transported short-haul by farmers to local landlords.

Surplus Sold Locally and Transhipped

Next let us discuss what happened to the surplus food which was sold in local market towns. It produced complex patterns which rippled across the Roman economy. But for the sake of simplicity, I should like to isolate four destinations: (a) the city of Rome, (b) the very large cities of Alexandria, Antioch and Carthage, (c) other towns, particularly those accessible by river and sea, and (d) local market towns fed on the local surplus.

The City of Rome

The city of Rome in the first century A.D. had a population of probably 800,000-1,000,000 people.[11] We have calculated that c. 80,000 tonnes of wheat were distributed free of charge to 200,000 adult male citizens. The whole metropolitan population, at the minimum level of subsistence, needed 200,000-220,000 tonnes of wheat equivalent. This makes no allowance for animal fodder, spoilage and consumption above the minimum necessary for subsistence. I should stress that measuring in wheat equivalent is a convenient tactic, not a statement about how much wheat was eaten. There is much debate about that; but Garnsey's recent estimate, at 150,000 tonnes seems reasonable. The rest of minimum consumption, and any more on top, was consumed, I reckon, in relatively expensive (denarii per calorie) foods: wine, olive oil, market vegetables, milk, wheat, spices and luxuries. The state provided 80,000 tonnes of wheat equivalent; inhabitants had to buy at least 120-140,000 tonnes of wheat equivalent, at a minimum cost of 60-70 million HS.[12] This is worked out at farm-gate prices, that is, without any transport costs added, at 3 HS per modius of 6.55 kg. These calculations are inevitably both crude and speculative. My objective here is not accuracy, but a rough order of magnitude to tease out implications which might remain obscured without rough figures. These calculations take absolutely no account of minimum consumption of cloth, fuel and housing, of consumption above the minimum, nor on the other side, of state requisitions to feed soldiers and the emperor's Court. But they illustrate a point to which we shall return that the city of Rome acted as a huge magnet for trade in the Roman economy. It was by far the largest and wealthiest single market. Its supply involved and occasionally made huge fortunes.[13]

The city of Rome had a large population because it was the capital of a large empire. Its population was supported to a considerable extent out of taxation, by the distribution of free wheat, and by the expenditure of the emperor, his household and officials of the profits of empire. Rome was thus a consumer city on a large scale, in the sense that its inhabitants depended for their life-style not on the production of goods for export, but on the production of goods and services for political overlords and large absentee landlords who spent their taxes and rents within the city.

Alexandria, Antioch, Carthage

The other great cities of the Roman empire, Alexandria, Antioch and Carthage had also once been political capitals of powerful empires. While they remained capital cities, their populations were supported to a considerable extent by the local expenditure of taxes. But after the Roman conquest, that tax expenditure was by and large withdrawn and transferred to Rome. We might have expected them to decline. But decline does not seem to have occurred. In Roman times, each probably had a population in the region of 250-500,000 people. The supporting evidence for these figures is flimsy, especially if we want precise numbers, but it is sufficient overall, I think, to justify the rough orders of magnitude.[14]

The existence of these very large cities is very important for our picture of the Roman economy. They did not live off the local expenditure of taxes, or not to a significant extent relative to their size. They were each the residences of large provincial grandees and heavily involved in the transmission of taxes from the provinces to Rome; doubtless they derived some of their wealth from rentier expenditure and from entrepôt business. But they were too large to be dependent on rentier business alone. They were too large to be fed from a locally produced surplus, especially because they were surrounded by ancillary settlements. The land in the immediate vicinity of the cities, like land round Rome, must have commanded premium rents, and therefore was devoted to crops of higher value than cereals.[15] Cereal production for these large cities must have been pushed out well beyond the immediate vicinity. In addition, the cities had to buy some of their staples from a distance. It seems reasonable to conclude that they gained a considerable part of their money by manufacture (crafts) and by commerce. These very large cities were not primarily consumer towns, they had to earn money with which to pay for their food by producing and selling their own products.

These very large cities were on or near the sea. That was no accident. The Mediterranean was a Roman lake, and for nearly three hundred years after the accession of Augustus, it was virtually free from pirates. Such security must have encouraged trade.[16] In addition, relatively cheap transport by sea (more about that later) must have made it possible to move sizeable quantities of wheat, wine and olive oil by boat around and across the Mediterranean.

Our problem is to estimate how much was moved and in what directions. So far we have isolated only two (perhaps three) target populations fed to a significant extent from outside their immediate locality. The city of Rome was fed partly by taxation (and rent) in kind, partly by private trade. The frontier armies were perhaps fed in part by taxation in kind. Finally, the very large cities of Alexandria, Antioch and Carthage which were involved as entrepôts in the transmission of taxes, but which were too large to be fed by the farmers in their immediate hinterland and which were centres of commerce and craft manufacture.

Other Market Towns

What other forces moved staples outside the immediate area of their production? At this point, I want to advance the view that the bulk of Roman staples transported in non-local trade between towns (other than Rome and the very large cities already mentioned), moved because of chance fluctuations in the size of harvests. Table 1 illustrates this point. It gives modern national statistics for wheat production from fourteen countries which were once part of the Roman empire.[17] Wheat was the dominant crop. Crops of other grains fluctuated similarly. Wine and olive oil production fluctuated even more. These wheat production figures were the earliest which I could find for such a wide range of countries. The introduction of modern selected seeds, fertilisers and iron ploughs had probably already reduced crop fluctuations in some countries.

Two items in the modern figures deserve special comment: first, in recent times, as in antiquity, Egypt was exceptional, not only for its high fertility, but also for the regularity or low variability of its wheat crop. Secondly, in many countries, especially in the southern and eastern Mediterranean, where rainfall is lowest, the variation between the size of each crop was considerable. At this point, I should stress that the figures in Table 1 are national figures from whole states; some of the statistics are probably unreliable (who counted and how?); but above all, national figures cancel out the much larger fluctuations of harvest which occurred in small districts. Peasants coped with these fluctuations, with glut and with shortage, partly through debt and credit, partly by storage in granaries, partly by changes in body-weight. In years of shortage, many of them starved.

The implications of unpredictable local harvests for the trade and transport of staples was considerable. One great difference between modern and Roman marketing systems lay in the absence of any regular routes of large-scale exchange between regions specializing in the production of an agricultural surplus and regions specializing in the production of manufacturers. The lines of ancient trade in staples produced by local glut and famine were unpredictable. The information available about markets must have been scant, distorted by rumour and difficult to trust. If glut occurred, there was no competent organization of merchant ships, finance or credit, ready waiting to carry the unpredicted surplus away. In times of famine, reciprocally, it was difficult to secure supplies, and the capacity to pay for them was limited by the scale of local bigwigs' generosity, and by the poverty of most consumers.[18] Medium-range trade in staples, therefore, was usually carried round in small ships by small-time merchants.

Any estimate is speculative. And the amount of food imported must have differed considerably between land-locked, riverine and coastal towns. In Table 2, I have arbitrarily set the level of these middle-range imports at 10% of urban needs. This may seem too high. But the target population, when food was scarce, was not merely the urban population but country folk as well. And some towns may have

Table 1

ANNUAL VARIATIONS OF WHEAT YIELDS (1921-30) IN FOURTEEN
MEDITERRANEAN COUNTRIES ONCE PARTS OF THE ROMAN EMPIRE*

a	b	c	d	e
Country	Average yield	Range	Mean annual variation around the mean	Average interannual variation
	kg/ha	(mean = 100)	per cent	per cent
Egypt	1710	92-110	5	12
Spain	904	86-113	8	17
Italy	1200	79-124	11	21
Cyprus	740	77-124	12	18
Bulgaria	1005	84-127	13	27
Greece	620	74-123	13	13
France	1420	89-122	14	19
Tunisia	400	57-122	16	67
Portugal	660	70-127	17	32
Algeria	540	61-143	18	47
Yugoslavia	1080	70-137	20	34
Syria and Lebanon	750	55-152	20	42
Turkey	840	65-135	21	19
Cyrenaica	269	[0]-279	(two years crop failure makes this calculation impossible)	

*From the *International Yearbook of Agricultural Statistics 1922-38*

For five countries the figures are from 1925-34, or 1929-38, because earlier figures
were not available.

NOTE that such national statistics are liable to gross error; they are national figures
and so disguise much greater regional variations.

regularly imported wine and olive oil rather than bulky wheat, from neighbouring market towns without causing a large rise in prices. Once such middle-range intra-regional trade in staples is taken into account, the estimate at 10% of urban minimum consumption seems plausible – even so it may not be right. It is time to desert quantification for qualitative impressions. My impression is that Roman inter-town trade in staples was by and large a topping up operation, the satisfaction of a marginal demand, a transfer of an occasional surplus to places where there was an unpredicted need. 'Traders', wrote Philostratus in his life of Apollonius of Tyana (4.32), 'roam from sea to sea looking for some market which is badly stocked'.

Long-Distance and Middle-Range Transport of Staples

In Table 2, I have attached rough estimates to the arguments advanced. I calculate middle-range and long-distance deliveries of staples alone as at least 460,000 tonnes of wheat equivalent per year. This estimate is based on minimum subsistence, and assumes for measurement purposes only, that staples were all in wheat. In so far as consumption, particularly in the city of Rome, and in the large cities was above minimum subsistence, or if urban populations were more than 10% of the total population, or if the population of the empire as a whole was more than fifty million, and if towns got more than 10% of their basic food on average from other towns, then these figures would have to be changed upwards. And *vice versa*. All in all, I think that the estimate of 460,000 tonnes wheat equivalent transported middle- and long-range is on the low side.

Its total value, at farm gate prices (i.e. without significant transport costs), say at 3 HS per *modius* of 6.55 kg, was 210 million HS per year, and much more if we take into account that much of it in fact consisted of higher priced olive oil and wine, not wheat. By this simple base calculation, we can see that, in aggregate, very large sums were involved in the sale and transport of staples outside their immediate district of production. How much of this large sum stuck to the fingers of intermediaries as it passed through the hands of merchants? How much of the large aggregate moved in big chunks through the granaries and store-rooms of large merchants?

Trade in goods other than staples is not directly within the purview of this essay. But the division is artificial. The sale and shipment of staples provided the basic framework of shipping, credit and quayside arrangements which could then be used for other foods and goods. Traded goods and fine foods travelled as supplementary cargo or as return cargo on ships carrying staples. Higher value, lower volume goods (textiles, spices, leather), provided merchants with their greatest profits. In addition, bulky goods, such as construction materials (bricks, timber), pots, metals, fuel could best be moved by boat. Such cargoes were of high volume and low unit value but they increased turnover and the use of harbour facilities. Trade in staples and non-staples were as intimately involved with each other as were short-haul and longer-range trade and transport. We consider this next.

TABLE 2

Hypothetical Minimum Estimates of Food Transport
Each Year in the Roman Empire

A. SHORT-HAUL

Food taken from countryside to nearby market towns and consumed there.

Assumptions:
1) urban population was 10% of empire's total population (50 million), plus metropolitan population of Rome, Alexandria, Antioch and Carthage (say 2 million)
2) minimum food intake was 220 kg wheat equivalent per person/year

				In tonnes wheat equivalent
A_1	Calculate:	10% x 50,000,000 x 220 kg	=	1,100,000 tonnes
A_2		plus local supply of the four metropolitan cities at say 100,000 for each x 220 kg (see note 25)	plus	88,000 tonnes
A_3		but see B_1	minus	110,000 tonnes
		Total Short-Haul (minimum estimate)		1,078,000 tonnes

B. MEDIUM-RANGE TRANSPORT

B_1	Transport to other market towns for fluctuating and unpredictable demand; say 10% of minimum urban need (A_1)	=	110,000 tonnes
B_2	Intra-regional food supply of three metropolitan cities (Alexandria, Antioch, Carthage), say 700,000 people x 220 kg (note A_2 above)	=	150,000 tonnes
B_3	Intra-regional, non local but Italian supply to Rome (see A_2 and $C_{1\ 2}$) say 150,000 x 220 kg	=	33,000 tonnes
B_4	Premium trade in wine and oil		considerable
B_5	Non local supplies to armies		?
B_6	Rents in kind		negligible?
			>295,000 tonnes

C. LONG-RANGE TRANSPORT

C_1	Taxes in kind sent to Rome (200,000 recipients of wheat dole x 60 *modii* of 6.55 kg)	=	80,000 tonnes
C_2	Market supply of wheat, wine and oil to Rome (total population say 1,000,000 x 220 kg minus ($1/4$ x A_2) B_3 and C_1	=	85,000 tonnes
C_3	Premium trade all over Mediterranean		?
C_4	Rents in kind		negligible
			>165,000 tonnes

Short-Haul Transport and Local Urban Consumption

Most of the agricultural surplus was transported by farmers to their local market town and consumed there. This conclusion follows from my general argument that there was no large-scale regional specialization in agricultural production, and no staple lines of inter-town trade in staples, except to Rome and the three other very large cities. All other towns lived mostly off the produce of their immediate hinterland. This follows from my lowish estimate of inter-town trade (tentatively set at 10% of minimum urban demand for food). But even if we double the value of medium-range, inter-town trade in staples, it would not upset the general conclusion. In Table 2, I estimated that two thirds of all food transported to local market towns was consumed there (1.1 million out of 1.5 million tonnes wheat equivalent per year).

The economic significance of this short-haul surplus did not stop with its consumption. Most consumers had to pay for their food.[19] In order to earn money, urban consumers typically either provided services to local peasants and townsmen or they made goods. The goods they made went either

(a) back to local peasants, or
(b) to fellow townsmen, or
(c) further afield to other urban markets.

What was the relative size of these three markets? The sheer mass of the agricultural population (>80% of the total) and their differentiation (some lived well above minimum subsistence) means that we should not undervalue peasants' aggregate consumption of urban goods and services (a). Townsmen's capacity to consume (b) and (c) was set by their productivity. In general, I assume that small units of production with negligible capital investment kept urban productivity low, so that townsmen's productivity was roughly similar, on average, to peasants' productivity and consumption, with similar and considerable variation. Except for rentier landowners and their retainers, therefore, there was in general a low ceiling to urban purchasing capacity (per capita), and local products (b) presumably competed with imported products (c) for the market.

Three points can be briefly made. First, one of the main stimuli to inter-urban trade was taxation. It created a necessity within each town to sell local food or to produce goods which could either be sent to Rome or sold to frontier garrison towns, where soldiers spent their pay, or to produce goods which could be fed into the network of interconnected middle-range markets. Total state revenues equalled about 800 million HS = 1.8 million tonnes wheat equivalent in the mid-first century A.D. Some of this was collected in kind, some no doubt spent near its point of collection. Even if only one half was spent away from its region of origin and had to be earnt back, its impact on trade was considerable.

Secondly, Rome itself and the great cities of Alexandria, Antioch and Carthage were high cost zones within the economy. The population of Rome itself was helped out by state subsidies; otherwise, I imagine, its population would not have been able to earn enough to pay for food, once transport prices and transaction costs had been added. But the populations of the other great cities did earn money with which to pay for imported food. That point has already been made. What I want to stress now is slightly different. The model which I have been developing here is too flat. There were in fact different zones within the Roman economy, fertile zones, arid zones, river accessible and land-locked zones, high cost and low cost zones, mining, pastoral and arable zones. This differentiation in physical endowment, in population densities and in costs, complemented taxation, its exaction and expenditure, in providing the dynamic for trade.

Thirdly, townsmen's capacity to produce goods cheaply and to sell their products outside their locality fixed their capacity to buy other towns' handmade goods and staples. The division of staples from non-staple foods and goods is not merely artificial, it is a definite obstacle to the understanding of the Roman economy.

My objective in the first part of this essay has been to construct a rough model which will show up some probable relationships within the Roman economy. For tactical convenience, I divided the transport of staples into short-haul, middle-range and long-distance. I have tried to show how they tied in with each other, and with the production and sale of goods. I have also touched on some probable relationships between town and country, taxes and trade, entrepôts and major urban markets. One advantage of such a model is that it prevents us from being overwhelmed by the sheer impossibility of coming to any conclusions at all because of the fragmentary character of the surviving testimony.

Two disadvantages need to be stressed. First, the model deals with the main outlines of probability; it does not deal with the complexities of local variations, nor with variations over time. I need hardly emphasise the importance of such variations, to say nothing of the numerous archaeological finds which do not fit in neatly with rational economic expectations. As a tactic of intellectual discovery, my model assumes economic rationality. In fact, I suspect, Romans often behaved economically irrationally or were motivated by factors and prices which we do not know about. Much of the past is irrecoverable. Secondly, I have rather rashly tried to quantify some elements in the discussion. These quantities are experimental. I hope that they are not wildly wrong, but several are closer to guesses than to fact. They should be treated with extreme caution, and if they are cited, they should be cited with some qualification. They are invitations to argument and discussion.

Finally, some comparative evidence may help put these calculations about Roman transport and trade into perspective. Perkins estimated that in fourteenth century China, about 20-30% of agricultural produce was traded, and that about 7-8% was transported outside its local district of production.[20] At first sight, such calculations may fill the Roman historian with envy. It is obviously impossible to make any such calculations for Roman trade, by the traditional techniques of patient, inductive empiricism. We simply cannot build such structures from archaeological finds in scattered sites and from literary or epigraphical fragments. And how, from the evidence available, could we make fine distinctions or measure changes in the volume of Roman transport and trade, say between 6% and 8% of gross agricultural product? Yet such a change, from 6% to 8%, implies growth by one third. Instead, we have to be content with rough impressions and crude indices, such as the volume of archaeological finds at Roman levels, the number of coins found, the size of ships. We can fit them into competing models of the Roman economy and judge which we find most convincing.

Even rough figures may help us in our choice of models. A minimum estimate of gross agricultural product in the Roman empire (Population x Minimum Subsistence + Seed) equals about 18 million tonnes wheat equivalent.[21] 7% of that is 1.3 million tonnes. By contrast, in Table 2, I have estimated Roman medium-range and long-distance transport of staples at 0.5 million tonnes wheat equivalent. But that calculation took no account of the higher value of some staples (wine, olive oil), and no account of trade in non-staple foods, in luxuries, textiles, construction materials, fuel, leather, metals and pots. Can we estimate the actual total value of Roman middle-range and long-distance trade? I do not think so. And yet, if only one half of the 1.8 million tonnes wheat equivalent raised in taxes was matched by middle-range and long-distance trade, then the total volume of Roman trade approached fourteenth century Chinese proportions.

II. *The Cost of Ships and of Transport*

I turn now to two issues of detail: the cost of cargo ships and of transport in the Roman world. The first is an important element in the rough model. I have argued that the value and volume of long-distance and middle-range transport and trade in staples, non-staple foods and goods in the Roman empire in the first two centuries A.D. was huge. They must have contributed greatly to the prosperity of the towns through which they passed. I now argue that ships on major trade routes were often large, and that they were so expensive to build, and valuable to own, especially when laden, that members of the Roman social elite were probably involved in their ownership. Ships like mines offered real economies of scale and required a considerable concentration of risk capital.

Roman ships were expensive. We can tell this by comparing their method of construction with that of later ships, both in the Mediterranean and in north-western Europe. Roman merchant ships were built outer shell first. Each external plank was joined to the next by mortice and tenon joints and by wooden dowels (trenails). Copper bolts were sometimes but not often used in the period 200 B.C.-A.D. 100. They were used more often later. The outer shell was then sometimes supplemented by a second internal skin of wooden planks, and the whole shell was finally strengthened by an internal frame. Protection against marine borers was increased by lead sheathing below the water-line, which made ships slower and more expensive. The main tools of construction were the saw, the adze and the plane. There are no known technical improvements in Roman ship construction between 200 B.C. and A.D. 400. In summary, Romans built quite large merchant ships with simple tools very carefully, "like fine pieces of furniture".[22]

Later Roman ships (increasingly perhaps from about A.D. 400 onwards), Byzantine ships and northern European ships in mediaeval times were, by contrast, built up from the internal frame – what is called skeleton construction as against the earlier Roman shell constructions. Once a strong skeleton had been built, outer planks were fixed by iron bolts and nails to the frame, to form a waterproof cladding. The gaps between the outer planks were caulked. In the fully developed northern European skeleton-built ship, the outer planks were fastened one over the other, clinker-style. I should stress that the date of the transition is uncertain and probably evolved over a considerable period. But there are distinct signs of a change towards skeleton construction in two wrecks dated about A.D. 400 and A.D. 600.

Two differences between the two methods of ship construction deserve emphasis. First, skeleton construction needed far fewer man-hours of skilled carpentry – iron bolts and nails instead of mortice and tenon joints. Secondly, in skeleton construction, the survival of the ship depended more upon the strength of the skeleton than on the condition of the exterior hull. This involved using heavier wood for the frame than in shell construction. Skeleton construction also involved higher repair costs to the outer skin in the course of a ship's life. But overall, the capital costs of skeleton construction should have been significantly less than shell construction.

The Size of Roman Merchant Ships

Let us now consider the size of Roman merchant ships. Our evidence is of four kinds: first, archaeological remains; secondly, occasional comments in ancient Roman histories, in legal texts and literature; thirdly, comparative evidence from other societies at a similar technical level; fourth, analytical thinking. Let us begin with the archaeological finds.

Underwater archaeologists have tracked down perhaps 800 sea wrecks from classical times, of which about 550 can be dated. I have argued elsewhere that these dated wrecks provide a good preliminary index of the relative incidence of ship-sailings in successive periods.[23] The evidence confirms our general supposition that ship-sailing was more frequent between 200 B.C. and A.D. 200 than ever before or in the next thousand years. This index is obviously crude; the location of dated wrecks largely depends on the activities of local enthusiasts; the eastern Mediterranean is under-represented; pirates may have sunk some ships; and finally, if ships sailed more in one period across the open sea than along the coast, then their traces are less likely to have been found. These are real problems, but even so I think the correlation roughly holds: the more sailings, the more wrecks, and more wrecks because of more trade.

Only very few of all these wrecks, one or two dozen, have been thoroughly investigated. Clearly, therefore, we cannot deduce from them a typical merchant ship size for Roman times. Nevertheless, I want to draw attention to seven well-studied wrecks listed in an excellent synoptic article by P. Pomey and A. Tchernia.[24]

Find-spot	Date by Century	Estimated Size (tonnes burden)
Mahdia	early 1 B.C.	240
Madrague de Giens	mid 1 B.C.	350
Albenga	1 B.C.	450
St Tropez	2 A.D.	>200
Torre Sgarrata	end 2 A.D.	210
Marzarmeni I	3 A.D.	>200
Isola delle Correnti	dk	350

The consistency of this archaeological evidence suggests that Romans commonly built ships in the range 200-350 tonnes burden, from the last century B.C. onwards.

A legal text, dating from the second century A.D. seems to bear this out but only in part and ambiguously. Those who built ships and used them to help supply the city of Rome with wheat were freed of other civic obligations, provided that their ships were of at least 330 tonnes burden or that they had several ships of that total, each of at least 65 tonnes burden (*Dig.* 50.5.3, Scaevola). The city of Rome by the end of the last century B.C. had a population of close on one million people. Supplying it with food, clothing, fuel, and other consumables, to say nothing of building materials, must have generated a huge amount of sea-borne traffic. A low estimate, of food alone at 220 kg wheat equivalent per head, is 220,000 tonnes per year.[25]

The demand for wheat in the city of Rome, effectively subsidised by the state, was very stable. If large ships were common, we should have expected them to have been engaged predominantly in bringing wheat to Rome, from the regular wheat-exporting provinces, namely Egypt, north Africa and Sicily. Yet this legal text suggests (as does another: *Dig.* 3.6, Ulpian) that not enough ships of over 300 tonnes burden could be found; some ship-owners engaged in supplying Rome with wheat used small ships of 65 tonnes burden.[26]

At the other extreme, there is some literary evidence for very large ships of 1000 tonnes burden or more. The three largest ancient merchant ships recorded may have been, by conservative estimates, roughly 1200-1900 tonnes burden.[27] Two of these were built by the order of monarchs, and were in no sense ordinary ships. The first was a white elephant, built by a local king of Syracuse before 221 B.C., of about

1900 tonnes burden. It was purportedly a wheat-carrying ship, designed in part by Archimedes. It had more than 700 crew, including marines, but excluding oarsmen; it also had luxurious living quarters for passengers and their horses, and sophisticated armament, including huge catapults. But after it had been built, the king discovered that there were no harbours large enough to take it without damage or risk, so he gave it as a present to the king of Egypt. The ship sailed once to Alexandria, where it was beached (Athenaeus 206ff.).

The second was built in the reign of Caligula (in A.D. 40) to carry an obelisk and its pedestal from Alexandria to Rome. It was of about 1300 tonnes burden.[28] This ship also sailed only once, and was more useful sunk than afloat, since it served as the foundation for one of the moles of the new harbour at Ostia. 'Nothing', wrote Pliny, 'more amazing than this ship has been seen at sea' (*Natural History* 16.201). His astonishment makes it clear that ships of that size were unusual.

The third large ship has been the subject of much scholarly controversy. It is described at the beginning of a satirical essay about the variety of human wishes by Lucian, who wrote in the second century A.D. An 'exceptionally large' wheat ship was on its way from Alexandria to Rome, when it was blown off course. Seventy days after it set sail, it put into the Piraeus, the port of Athens. Lucian described the ship as 120 cubits (*pecheis*) long, 30 cubits broad, and 29 cubits at its deepest part (*The Ship* 5). Modern interpretations of these figures vary enormously; its tonnage has been estimated (to cite only six findings) at 1177, 1228, 2157, 2672, 5786 and 6440 tonnes burden.[29] In my opinion, all these estimates seem improbably large. Lucian's statement: 'there's an army of sailors on board, they say. They say that it carries enough wheat to feed all Attica for a year' (*ibidem*) sounds like rhetorical exaggeration, fantasy not fact. It should discourage us from taking the figures cited above as accurate measurements.

I would not have spent so much time on these sea monsters, but for the fact that influential scholars have thought that huge ships of 1000 tonnes burden were regularly engaged in carrying grain to the city of Rome in the first two centuries A.D.[30] On the literary and archaeological evidence cited, such a conclusion seems illegitimate. Nor is it strengthened by comparative evidence. Ships of 1000 tonnes burden and over were regularly built for the cross Atlantic trade, and for northern European trade with India and China only from about 1800. Although ships of over 1,000 tonnes burden were built in Genoa as early as the fifteenth century, they were rare. In the early eighteenth century, the average size of ships trading from England to India was 440 tonnes burden.[31] Ships on these long-distance routes were, of course, selected for size. The average size of all sea-going vessels was significantly lower. For example, in the beginning of the eighteenth century, the average size of all ships entering Boston, Chesapeke and Barbados was only 50, 90 and 57 tons burden.[32] Such evidence, incidentally, casts serious doubt on Casson's much quoted conclusion: 'the smallest craft the ancients reckoned suitable for overseas shipping was 70-80 tons burden'.[33] That is both intrinsically implausible, and based as it happens on an inscription (about the harbour regulations at Thasos from the third century B.C.) which has an unreadable gap where the vital numeral should be.[34]

Let me go back briefly to the comparative evidence, and in particular to those known giants of Mediterranean commerce in early modern times, Genoa and Venice. In the middle of the fifteenth century, the average size of large merchant ships (>380 tonnes) at Genoa was 630 tonnes, and the largest ship was over 1000 tonnes.[35] By contrast, the largest ships calling in at Marseille and Barcelona in the mid-fifteenth century was less than 500 tonnes burden. Venice, a century later, in 1559 had only 36 or 38 ships of more than 240 tonnes burden, of which the largest was 720 tonnes.[36] And in the same period, the average size of ships using the Spanish Mediterranean ports was only about 75 tonnes.[37]

Where does all this lead us? The Romans had the technical capacity to build very large ships (of over 1000 tonnes burden). There is no evidence that they commonly did so. Understandably, because if they were blown off course, it was difficult to find harbours for them. Large ships were very expensive to build, and even more expensive to lose if they sunk with a full cargo. Later evidence and Roman evidence suggests that most Roman merchant ships were small (<200 tonnes and even <80 tonnes). Even on important trade routes, and even if the city of Rome was their market, many ships probably sailed there from small ports in Spain, southern France, Sicily and north Africa. They had to put in at small ports. And yet, the archaeological evidence from shipwrecks is compelling: ships of 250–450 tonnes burden were built from the last century B.C. Shipowners taking wheat to Rome gained tax exemptions only if they owned ships which either in one unit or in several exceeded 330 tonnes.

Can our knowledge of the size of Roman ships, however imperfect, be used to improve our understanding of Roman economic history? I think it can, especially if we can estimate how much Roman ships cost. The main obstacle here is that there is no surviving literary evidence about ship prices. That may not be an insuperable problem. We know that the Romans built some ships of 250–450 tonnes burden by the expensive shell method of construction, with the hull planks fixed one on top of the other by mortice and tenon joints. We know that post-medieval ships were built by the cheaper skeleton method of construction. As a sighting shot, therefore, just to give us a rough order of magnitude, let us look at the price of building 400 tonne ships (a) in Genoa in the mid-fifteenth century and (b) in England in the seventeenth century. I choose these two examples simply because evidence on ship prices there is available.

Needless to say such comparisons pose considerable difficulties. I am not at all sure that I am comparing like with like, and besides the prices of Genoese and English ships varied widely; but then so, I imagine, did the price of Roman ships. Shipbuilders always have to choose between, on the one hand high capital cost plus a long life, and on the other hand lower capital cost and a short life for the ship, and between strength and buoyancy. For the moment, let us ignore variation and take average prices. But prices in Genoese lire and £ sterling will not help us. So we adopt the standard practice for translating prices between different pre-industrial societies and convert current coin into tonnes of wheat. The justification for this conversion is that the prices of so many goods and wages co-vary broadly with wheat prices. And I must stress again that we are looking for rough orders of magnitude only, not for exact prices. The final jump in what must by now seem an endless series of speculations is to convert tonnes of wheat into Roman currency. I take the standard price to be 3 HS per modius of 6.55 kg. That price is much too low for the city of Rome and perhaps too high for some regions of the empire. What is the result of all these calculations? The average price of building and fitting out a 400 tonne merchant ship in Genoa in the mid-fifteenth century was 772 tonnes of wheat or 354,000 HS (N=5). The equivalent English price in the seventeenth century was 628 tonnes of wheat or 288,000 HS (N=6).[38]

Now I have taken the average cost of only eleven ships, and the variation between their costs was considerable. The price of wheat varied, and so did construction costs. Further research is necessary to check that such construction costs were normal. Nonetheless the figures seem striking. A Roman ship of 400 tonnes burden, expensively built by the method of shell construction, probably cost, if my calculations are at all correct, at least 250-400,000 HS. Its cargo, if it was wheat, was worth, at the same price, another 185,000 HS. If wheat was worth more, especially when delivered at Rome, or if the cargo was more valuable, then the total ship's value, including freight, was more than 400,000-600,000 HS.

We can go further in an analysis of Roman transport and trade. We have already calculated that Rome's population of about one million people consumed at least 220 kg wheat equivalent each (220,000 tonnes). That was a minimum. We must add extra food, luxuries, fodder for animals, building stone and timber, bricks and mortar, paving stones and fuel. The volume of imports to Ostia, Rome's port and to the riverside quays of the city, some 35 km upstream, must have been huge. What volume of shipping was involved? That obviously depends on the number of voyages which each ship made. Two factors deserve particular mention: first, it was customary for Roman cargo ships to stay in port for four months during winter (Vegetius, *On Military Matters* 4.39).[39] Secondly, sailing ships had to stay a considerable time in port, partly because of weather bunching: they tended to arrive all together with a fair wind and wait to leave together when the wind set fair. And this inevitably prolonged average turnaround times.[40] If we allow ships two trips on average to Ostia each year (less from Egypt, more from Sicily), then the capital cost of the merchant fleet provisioning Rome with staples alone (notionally 275 ships of 400 tonnes at say 300,000 HS per ship) was 80 million HS. Once we include the transport of non-foods and add in the value of river boats bringing the food upstream, 100 million HS seems a conservative, minimum estimate.

In sum, supplying the city of Rome involved food and goods of very high aggregate value (enough food for minimum subsistence alone was worth 65 million HS per year at farm-gate wheat prices). This food was transported in ships, each of which cost a lot (say 300,000 HS per 400 tonnes). The total capital value of ships involved in supplying the city of Rome alone probably equalled over 100 million HS, that is the minimum fortunes of 100 senators. The sums involved, especially in large ships, were so substantial that it was likely to have involved those Romans with substantial capital to invest and to put at risk. They probably split the risk by taking shares in ships (Plutarch, *Cato the Elder* 21); that enabled Romans of middling means to participate in maritime trade; it did not diminish the total capital involvement. The total risk capital invested in trade and transport to Rome, and in the rest of the Mediterranean, was very large. It did not equal investment in land, either in size or status, but because it was more risky, it was also probably more profitable to those who succeeded.

Transport Prices

Let us now turn to freight charges. Our best evidence, apparently, comes from Diocletian's Edict on Maximum Prices promulgated in Nicomedia in Asia Minor in A.D. 301. The Edict was widely publicised and set up on stone inscriptions in Greek and Latin; curiously it was often set out in Latin even in Greek-speaking provinces.[41] This is an important point in that it suggests symbolic display rather than effective price control. But more of that later. Well over 1000 prices survive from the Edict including 44 prices for sea transport. They run like this:

From Nicomedia to Thessalonika, for 1 military modius 8 denarii.
From Alexandria to Aquileia, for 1 military modius 24 denarii.

The price of wheat is also given. Thanks to Duncan-Jones we know that one military modius was equal to 1½ Italian *modii*, that is roughly 10 kg of wheat.[42] We can measure the distance between the ports named and work out a price – so many kg of wheat for each tonne/km, that is the price paid to carry one tonne one kilometre. The median price is 0.8 kg wheat per tonne/km, which seems very cheap, though prices vary considerably around that median.[43]

How were the transport prices fixed? It seems to me likely that they were calculated by measuring distances on a map or by taking distances between ports from a nautical gazetteer, similar to but more sophisticated than the local gazeteers which survive from the third and fourth centuries (such as the *Maritime Itinerary* and the *Gazeteer (Stadiasmos) of the Great Sea*). Diocletian's Edict was concerned with long voyages between provinces. The map which Dioletian's administrators used was fairly accurate. We can tell this, because to a significant extent, differences in prices for transport corresponded to actual differences in distances between ports. On the whole, with some notable exceptions, the more you paid, the further your goods could go. The correlation between distances and prices was 0.72; or put another way, distance accounted for just over half (52%) of the variance in prices. Indeed, the calculations which the Roman administrators executed were more subtle; the further your goods went, the lower the unit price of transport (the more km per denarius), although this fit was rougher and there were some serious discrepancies. In other words, there was a discount for very long voyages. The correlation between distance and cost per km was –0.47, a result which it would have been difficult to get by chance. In sum, we can admire the Roman administrators for their general accuracy, and even for subtlety in calculation, while being puzzled by some of their errors.

One contributory explanation of these calculations is that eastern administrators, stationed in Nicomedia, underestimated the length and breadth of the western Mediterranean. This is not the place to go into details. Suffice it to say that the prices given for transport in or through the Western Mediterranean were systematically lower than for the Eastern Mediterranean. These price differences cannot be explained, either by the volume of shipping travelling along the routes named (e.g. Carthage to Marseille), or by the extra length of the voyages. The easiest explanation is that Eastern officials thought that the Western Mediterranean was shorter than it was in reality.

We find a similar error in the geographies of Eratosthenes and Dicaearchus (reported by Strabo 2.4.2-4) in the third century B.C. But curiously enough, that error was corrected, overcorrected even, by other later geographers, Polybius, Strabo and by the great Ptolemy. They thought the western Mediterranean was longer (25% longer) than it is in reality and somewhat wider. It would be tempting, therefore, to suppose that the eastern administrators were using a very old map. But more realistically, I suspect the reason is that our surviving geographical sources are only a fraction of what existed. At any one time, several rival guides mixed accurate and misleading information from different traditions. It must have been very difficult for Roman geographers and administrators to decide between competing versions of the truth.

But the administrators' biggest source of error did not arise from the map's distortions, but from using a map, any map, as the basis of calculations for maximum prices of transport. If Diocletian's officials had stepped out of their offices, onto the quayside, they would have discovered, I think, that a wide variety of factors, such as prevalent winds, the time of year, and the volume of trade made such a difference to the length, safety and predictability of a voyage, that it must have been reflected in differential prices. Yet the maximum prices given in the Edict make no allowance for the possibility that prices on busy routes should be lower than those on less frequented routes, and to out of the way ports. Nor was there any separate provision for journeys in summer and autumn, nor for return journeys with or against the wind. And wind made a lot of difference. For example, according to one estimate, the journey from Rome to Alexandria normally took 20-25 days, but the return voyage against the prevailing winds took 53-73 days.[44] But in the Edict, no account was taken of the impact of winds on the cost of a voyage. The Edict as a whole failed because it did not take the complexities of real life into account. For sea transport, it failed because it tried to impose the artificial unidimensional order of a map on a variegated world. I conclude, reluctantly, that the Edict on Maximum Prices is not a reliable guide to actual transport charges, either in AD 301, or in the previous three centuries.

The same logic can be quickly applied to land transport. The Edict proposed a maximum price of 20 dn per Roman mile for a cart load weighing 1200 Roman pounds. This led A. H. M. Jones to an influential conclusion – 'A wagon load of wheat doubled in price by a journey of 300 miles' and to his famous comparison based on a belief in the Edict's reliability: 'It was cheaper to ship grain from one end of the Mediterranean to the other than to cart it 75 miles'.[45] But once again, it is worth asking how can this price fit all circumstances? Going over a mountain pass cost much more than going over level ground. Jones' dramatic illustration that wheat doubled in price over 300 Roman miles (or rather 200 Roman miles, because the military modius measured $1\frac{1}{2}$ ordinary modii) is misleading on several counts.[46] First, oxen move at under 3 km per hour and work normally for only 5 hours a day; let us say that they go 16 km per day. My point is almost made. It would be very surprising if wheat transported by ox-cart only doubled in price in 30 days travel from the point of departure. That is all the way from London to Newcastle, and in the eighteenth century, coal brought by sea from Newcastle to London cost at least five times as much in London as it did at the pit-head.[47] Secondly, the oxen and their driver would consume half the load, or its equivalent on their journey there and back. Put another way, charges for ox-wagon transport increase with distance.

I have tried to show that Diocletian's Edict is an unreliable guide to actual prices. What can be rescued? Perhaps if the details of the Edict are wrong, nevertheless the broad relativities are right. Here we face a common logical difficulty. The test of the acceptability of the ratios between the cost of transport by land, river and sea is comparative evidence. But if we can accept ancient evidence only if it accords with comparative evidence, and reject it if it diverges widely, why bother with the ancient evidence? I leave that methodological doubt on one side. Let us take the mean values of Diocletian's Edict (i.e. let us ignore variation), and add in a few bits of assorted evidence from Egypt). We find the following rough ratios:

> 10 units of cost per tonne/km for sea transport
> 60 units of cost per tonne/km for river transport
> 550 units of cost per tonne/km for land transport

and that roughly accords with comparavive evidence on relative transport prices from other societies.[48] This meant of course that no one in his economic right mind normally sent goods overland, if he could send them by river or sea.

On closer inspection, the contrast between sea transport prices and land transport prices is not so persuasive. In reality, most foods sent by sea originated at some distance from the quayside. Wheat had to be carted, unloaded, sold, stored, recarted, loaded into a ship, unloaded, stored, sold and carted again to its destination. In other words, long-distance trade involved a whole series of costs, typically including elements of both land transport and sea transport. But they also involved social organization – collection, distribution, sale, redistribution, the cost of credit and of covering the risk of loss. I am not at all sure that out of all these factors, transport costs were by themselves the largest or the critical element in determining the volume of long-distance and medium-range trade.

In famines, for example, wheat prices rose well above their normal level; to judge from scattered Roman evidence and much comparative data, twice the normal price or more was common in famines. According to Jones' dictum, then, wheat could have been sought overland to relieve a local famine within a radius of 300 Roman miles (444 km). But during a serious famine at Antioch in AD 362/3, this did not happen, or not until the emperor Julian intervened personally to secure large quantities of wheat from two towns only 50 and 100 km distant by land from Antioch.[49] These supplies had not been tapped previously, I suspect, because the need for them was both sudden and unusual; the organisation of men and animals to trade and transport staples in bulk overland was simply not available. It took an emperor's political power to marshal them.

In this essay, I have argued that the bulk of transport in the Roman empire was short-haul. By implication, most of it was overland. I readily acknowledge that transport overland was relatively expensive, and this higher cost was one factor inhibiting the growth of land-locked towns in antiquity. But it was only one factor of several. And as every Roman archaeologist knows, the expense of land transport did not prevent the widespread dispersion of Roman artefacts. Wine and oil were much more widely distributed than wheat, while the distribution of cloth was limited much more, I suspect, by the size of the market, by the capacity to purchase than by the costs of cartage. After all, according to Diocletian's Edict, if I can still use that source, a journey of 300 km overland added only 7% to the cost of medium quality wool (Edict 17 and 25). That surely presented no great obstacle to medium-range or to long-distance trade.

Complementarily, cheaper transport by sea was not enough to stimulate the unrestricted growth of coastal towns. That is the critical argument. As far as we know, very few Roman cities, located on river bank or sea-coast, grew in population significantly beyond the supportive capacity of their immediate hinterland. The well-known exceptions, Rome, Alexandria, Antioch and Carthage, are all important, and all grew large because they were capitals of empires. The economic growth of large cities in the Roman world was politically inspired. Their survival as cities, after their initial political functions had diminished, was a symptom of the Roman empire's economic sophistication.

London   KEITH HOPKINS

NOTES

1. See M. I. Finley, *The Ancient Economy* (1973); A. H. M. Jones, *The Roman Economy* (1974), see especially p. 30; P. Garnsey, K. Hopkins, C. R. Whittaker (edd.), *Trade in the Ancient Economy* (1983).

2. K. Hopkins, 'Taxes and trade in the Roman Empire (200 B.C.-A.D. 400)', *JRS* 70 (1980) 101ff.; Introduction to Garnsey et al. (n. 1); 'Economic Growth and Towns in Classical Antiquity', in P. Abrams et al. (edd.), *Towns in Societies* (1978) 35ff.; 'Brother-sister marriage in Roman Egypt', *Comparative Studies in Society and History* 22 (1980) 342-3 and, for example, on the inequality of land-holding in one large Egyptian village, see the data set out by H. Geremek, *Karanis, Communauté rurale de l'Égypte romaine, Archiwum Filologiczne* 17 (1969) 115; the ratio between the mean of the top 6% of village land-holdings by size and the mean of the bottom 59% was 13:1.

3. I define food surplus as all food produced over and above the demands of minimum subsistence and sufficient seed to replace that minimum subsistence. I define minimum subsistence as about 220 kg wheat equivalent per person/year, plus a small allowance of 30 kg wheat equivalent to provide minimal clothing, housing and fuel. This is only a rough approximation. See C. Clark and M. Haswell, *The Economics of Subsistence Agriculture* (1970) 62. Careful calculation taking into account the age structure of the population, body weight, temperatures and energies expended is impracticable.

4. Two qualifications are obviously necessary. I take no account here of transport for sale between villages; I do not doubt its significance but have no way of estimating its value or volume. Secondly, we should take account also of the transport of building materials – timber, stone, cement, bricks and tiles, clay for potteries, mineral ore for smelting and refined metals, timber for fuel. Even so, I suspect that the short-haul transport of food outweighed them all in tonnage and in tonnes/km.

5. The estimate of the empire's population at 50 million is on the low side. See K. J. Beloch, *Die Bevölkerung der griechischen-römischen Welt* (1886) 507. The estimate for the urban population at 10% is also on the low side, if we consider that Rome, Alexandria, Antioch and Carthage together had a population of about 2 million. Of course, not all the food was eaten as wheat; although wine and oil weigh less per calorie, their containers are heavy so that 220 kg may not be far out as a measure of the weight of minimum subsistence as transported.

6. In the fourth century A.D., citizens living at Rome received a free ration of pork as well as wheat and olive oil. See *C.Th.*14.4, SHA, *Septimius Severus* 18, *Aurelian* 35; Symmachus, *Letters* 10. 14 and 35. And in general, A. H. M. Jones, *The Later Roman Empire* (1964) 696ff.

7. Cf. Augustus, *Res Gestae* 15; for a brief discussion, see K. Hopkins, *Conquerors and Slaves* (1978) 96 and *cf.* note 11 below.

8. On deductions from military pay, see the commentary by R. O. Fink, *Roman Military Records on Papyrus* (1971) nos. 68-9; M. Speidel, 'The pay of the auxilia', *JRS* 63 (1973) 141ff. Jones (n. 6) 31 and 626ff.

9. Based on 300 leases analysed by G. Mickwitz, *Geld und Wirtschaft im römischen Reich* (1932) 120.

10. See the excellent commentary by L. Duchesne, *Liber Pontificalis* (1886) CL and 34. *P. Ital.* 3 referred to in the text above can be found in J. O. Tjäder, *Die nichtliterarischen lateinischen Papyri Italiens aus der Zeit 445-700* (1955).

11. On the population of Rome, see briefly Hopkins (n. 7) 96ff. For wheat consumption, P. Garnsey, 'Grain for Rome', in Garnsey et al. (n. 1) 118ff.; also L. Foxhall and H. A. Forbes, 'Sitometria. The role of grain as a staple food in classical antiquity', *Chiron* 12 (1982) 41ff. – the best article on the subject. However, they do not recognise the prescriptive element in FAO minimum standards (which are above actual consumption figures in several poor states); and their hypothetical typical household of 6 persons over 3 generations is demographically improbable in ancient conditions.

12. I calculate total demand as 1,000,000 population x 220 kg wheat equivalent person year. The high population estimate is balanced by the minimal estimate for food consumption, with no allowance for spoilage, waste, above-average consumption and fodder. Transport prices, profit and transaction costs would have more than doubled wheat prices in the capital (6 HS per modius or even 8 HS per modius). See the brief discussion by R. P. Duncan-Jones, *The Economy of the Roman Empire* (1974) 345-7.

13. See Petronius, *Satyricon* 76 on the fortune lost and made in the trade by his fictional anti-hero Trimalchio, and the comments made by Duncan-Jones (n. 12) 238ff. J. D'Arms tries to trace upper-class involvement in trade from fragile references in the literature and the similarity of names of known ex-slave traders and Roman aristocrats. I agree with him in substance, while regretting that the testimony he cites is far from proving his case (see his *Commerce and social standing in ancient Rome* (1981)). For a suggestive parallel, see E. A. Wrigley, 'A simple model of London's importance' in Abrams (n. 2) 215ff.

14. On the population of Alexandria, see Beloch (n. 5) 258-9 and P. M. Fraser, *Ptolemaic Alexandria* (1972) vol. 1, 90ff. and vol. 2, 171ff. On Antioch, see J. W. G. H. Liebeschuetz, *Antioch* (1972) 92-5, with the literature cited there. The ancient testimony is fragmentary: see Diodorus 17.52, Strabo 16.2.5 and Herodian 7.6 and 3.5.

15. I write 'must have' in an appeal to the logic of the situation, based partly on what is known from other large cities. See, for example, D. Ricardo, *On the Principles of Political Economy and Taxation* (1981), and P. Hall (ed.), *Van Thünen's Isolated State* (1966).

16. Suetonius, *Augustus* 98 records a story of sailors' gratitude to Augustus for the new peace and prosperity from trade. See J. Rougé, *L'organisation du commerce maritime en Mediterranée sous l'empire romain* (1966) 460ff.

17. Columns d and e give two different measures of fluctuations in the size of crops. Column d gives the average percentage deviation around the mean; column e measures the percentage change from each successive year to the next.

18. On the classical tradition of generosity by local grandees who felt an obligation to give back some of their wealth to the poor, see P. Veyne, *Le pain et le cirque* (1976) 209ff. Towns often appointed special officers (*sitonai*) to secure wheat for their inhabitants by imports. See A. H. M. Jones, *The Greek City* (1940) 217ff. But a gift, like the one recorded at Magnesia of 200,000 HS (*OGIS* 485) would have provided enough food for only 16,000 people for one month, if the price was 4 HS per modius; in a general shortage, prices would have been higher, and private generosity usually inadequate relative to the size of the population at risk. Moreover, local landowners often hoarded to make a profit out of the people's misery – see, for example, Philostratus, *vita Ap.* 1.15.

19. Absentee landowners and their households living off rents in kind are exceptions.

20. D. H. Perkins, *Agricultural Development in China 1368-1968* (1969) 115-36.

21. See Hopkins (n. 2) 119.

22. R. W. Unger, *The Ship in the Medieval Economy* (1980) 36-7. I am grateful to Mr Robin Craig of University College, London for his generous advice about naval history.

23. Hopkins (n. 2) 105-6.

24. 'Le tonnage maximum des navires de commerce romains', *Archaeonautica* 2 (1978) 233ff.

25. Some of Rome's food supplies must have come from around Rome itself and down the Tiber. I crudely reckon this at enough to feed 100,000 people at minimum subsistence. In the sixteenth century, when Rome's population was about 150,000 people, it relied significantly on imports by sea. See J. Delumeau, *La vie économique et sociale de Rome* (1959) II 521ff.

26. Pomey and Tchernia argue ingeniously (*a*) that these small ships were engaged primarily in coastal lightering, bringing wheat from the great port at Puteoli to Rome, and (*b*) that the regulation was the product of a particular crisis in the reign of Claudius (Suetonius, *Claudius* 18-19, Tacitus, *Annals* 12. 43), before the harbour at Ostia was built. Maybe. But the regulations persisted until the second century A.D.

27 Pomey and Tchernia (n. 24) 245-7.

28. *Ibidem.*

29. *Ibidem* and Rougé (n. 16) 69-70.

30. L. Casson, *Ships and Seamanship in the Ancient World* (1971) 173 and 183ff.; J. G. Landels, *Engineering in the Ancient World* (1980) 165-6; Unger (n. 22) 36.

31. See E. K. Chatterton, *The Old East Indiamen* (1933) 145, 178-9; H. B. Morse, *The East India Company Trading to China* (1926) vol. 1, 307ff.; vol. 2, 436ff.

32. J. F. Shepherd and G. M. Walton, *Shipping, Maritime Trade and the Economic Development of Colonial North America* (1972) 195-6.

33. Casson (n. 30) 171; cf. G. Rickman, *The Corn Supply of Ancient Rome* (1980) 123. Incidentally, Rickman (p. 10) believes that Romans ate on average 260 kg wheat (not wheat equivalent) per person per year (men, women and children). That's a lot of bread.

34. The original editor of the inscription, M. Launey, restored the gap with 'three thousand' talents (80 tonnes), but commented that four thousand, six thousand or seven thousand could each from an epigraphical viewpoint plausibly fill the gap ('Inscriptions de Thasos', *BCH* 57 (1933) 396). The main subsequent edition (*IG* XII suppl. p. 151 no. 348) brackets [three] thousand without noting Launey's alternative emendations.

35. J. Heers, *Gênes au XVe siècle* (1961) 273 and 639ff.

36. M. Aymard, *Venise, Raguse et le commerce du blé* (1966) 57-8.

37. F. Braudel, *The Mediterranean and the Mediterranean world in the age of Philip II* (1972) 304.

38. See Heers (n. 35) 288, 340 and 621-2; R. Davis, *The Rise of the English Shipping Industry* (1962) 338ff.; cf. R. G. Albion, *Forests and Sea Power* (1926) 90, 93; on wheat prices, see B. R. Mitchell, *Abstract of British Historical Statistics* (1962) 486ff. I took the average shipwrights' construction cost of six ships of over 230 measured tons built in England in the second half of the seventeenth century. The cost per measured ton (£6.5) was converted into tonnes burden (4/3), and I reckoned the cost of fitting out to be the same as in the English trade with southern Spain (2/3 of hull and rigging cost); so Davis 1962: 372-3, 378. The average price of wheat 1650-1699, I took to be £1.94 per quarter of 211 kg. Each element in this chain of calculation poses difficulties.

39. Casson (n. 30) 270-3; Rougé (n. 16).

40. Shepherd and Walton (n. 32) 198 cite average turn around times in Boston, Maryland and Virginia in the late seventeenth century as 36, 106 and 94 days. Cf. Select Papyri (Loeb Classical Library) 113 for delays at Ostia with Casson's comments (n. 30) 298.

41. M. Giacchero, *Edictum Diocletiani* (1974).

42. R. P. Duncan-Jones, 'The size of the modius castrensis', *ZPE* 21 (1976) 53-62.

43. The whole list of sea transport prices from Diocletian's Edict and distances between ports is set out in K. Hopkins, 'The Transport of Staples', *Eighth International Economic History Congress Budapest 1982* (1982) Table 1 85-6.

44. L. Casson, 'The Isis and her voyage', *TAPA* 81 (1950) 43-56, at 51; 'Speed under sail of ancient ships', *TAPA* 82 (1951) 136-48, at 145.

45. Jones (n. 6) 841-2, cited by Finley (n. 1) 126; Rickman (n. 33) 14; G. E. M. de Ste Croix, *The Class Struggle in the Ancient Greek World* (1981) 11.

46. Jones (n. 6) 841; Jones here apparently forgot that Diocletian's Edict was concerned with military modii (*castrenses*), then conventionally (cf. Hultsch) equated with two Italic modii; so his result should have been 'doubled in price by a journey of 150 [Roman] miles'. A result often cited, but not checked.

47. F. Braudel, *The Wheels of Commerce* (1983) 361.

48. See similarly Duncan-Jones (n. 12) 367-9.

49. Jones (n. 6) 445-6.

11. TRADE AND FRONTIERS OF THE ROMAN EMPIRE*

It is natural that Roman frontiers and frontier strategy should usually be examined from the standpoint of military dispositions. That is, after all, one of the main concerns of any frontier. But such accounts are notoriously unsatisfactory to military specialists, who often discover that the Romans could easily have established much better tactical and strategic locations if they had looked a bit harder.[1] This, in itself, suggests that, while Roman frontiers may have served a military function, yet military rationality is not necessarily – perhaps never – the overriding determinant of where a frontier is located. For frontiers are concerned with political power. And power may be exercised as much through social or economic controls as by military domination. Availability of resources, therefore, and trade or economic needs may offer a more comprehensive explanation both for the logic of frontier formation and for the eventual collapse. One has to say 'more comprehensive', because there is no reason why all frontiers should have identical explanations where local conditions differed and it is perhaps a misguided effort to search for a single, empire-wide 'Grand Strategy'.[2] Even the most cursory study of the *Notitia Dignitatum*, for example, will show that in the Later Roman Empire troop dispositions between Occident and Orient must have differed quite radically. This is what we should expect always to have been true to some extent.

A. Let me begin with three historical examples to illustrate the effect of frontiers upon local populations:-

1. In A.D. 70 an unusual drought in Germany lowered the water level of the Rhine which made the crossing of the river easier for Germans from the north bank, while at the same time causing lower harvest yields in both France and Germany – 'a smaller supply of grain and a greater number of consumers', (Tac. *Hist.* 4.26) put pressure on the frontiers. Soon after this at Cologne the German Tencteri, demanding restoration of their ancestral rights of free movement and settlement on either side of the Rhine, forced the Roman colony to repeal 'all taxes and restriction on trade' (Tac. *Hist.* 4.64-5).
2. A few years earlier, in A.D. 58, two Frisian chiefs moved their people into unoccupied military land along the Rhine and began to cultivate the soil. After vainly begging the Emperor Nero that they might possess this area as a new home, they were expelled. But other Germans, the Ampsivarii, in turn demanded the land, claiming that leaving land idle was wrong 'while men were starving' (Tac. *Ann.* 13.54-5).
3. In A.D. 17, this time beyond the frontiers in Southern Tunisia, the Musulami

leader, Tacfarinas, made what the Romans considered an insulting demand from the Emperor Tiberius, for land settlements for himself and his men within the Roman province, for which he was desperate enough to fight (Tac. *Ann.* 3.73). Once again the words of Tacitus suggest that the need was for unimpeded access to grain (Tac. *Ann.* 4.13).

The implication of these examples is the first general proposition I wish to put forward, namely, that *Roman frontiers frequently cut through zones of relative homogeneity* – and in particular of economic or social homogeneity. For this unoriginal starting point, there is nowadays a large literature in support. I am thinking of the work done on the La Tène *oppida* culture north of the Rhine by scholars such as Eggers, Will and others in Germany (recently excellently summarized by Wells) or by Filip in Central Europe.[3] Their work has proved the ambiguity of the folk on either side of the northern frontiers. At the time when Romans and Germans met on the Rhine, there were the *Völker zwischen Germanen und Kelten*, as the title of the book by Hachmann, Kossack and Kuhn puts it.[4] The Germanic and Suevic peoples who reached the hill country of Westfalia, Hessen and Saxony were thus partially 'Celticized' by the La Tène Celts before, or just as, they met the Roman imperial armies. Conversely the Belgic Tungri and Treveri within the Roman frontiers claimed German origins (Caes. *Bell. Gall.* 2.4, 8.25; cf. Tac. *Germ.* 2.5), while there were apparently whole sections of people inside Gaul called *Germani Cisrhenani*, of whom it is difficult to tell whether they were Germans, Celts or what – people familiar to us in Roman frontier history like the Usipites, Tencteri, Ubii, Sugambri, and so on – whom Hawkes thinks to have been true border folk.[5] The Mattiaci, for instance, who are later found at Metz, were originally probably linked to the *oppidum* called Mattium at Altenberg in the Wetterau until overrun and partially displaced by the Chatti (Tac. *Ann.* 1.56). Ariovistus, says Caesar, spoke Celtic *longinqua consuetudine* (*BG* 1.47.4) and the people of Baden-Würtemberg in the *Agri Decumates* are said by Tacitus to have been 'Gallic' (*Germ.* 29.4).

Further East in the Pannonian provinces of the middle Danube our information is roughly the same, if we look at the regions of Moravia and Bohemia. There the Celtic *oppida* culture had flourished and is traceable from the Danube 'knee' as far as the North-Eastern Carpathians and the Russian Ukraine, where it came into violent contact with the Dacians and Sarmatians. That clash resulted in the ultimate displacement of Celtic groups like the Boii, Cotini and Osi, forcing them to spill over into Northern Pannonia. All this, too, was beginning to happen at just about the time the Romans were being sucked into affairs in Illyricum, where both Caesar and Augustus believed as a matter of urgency that they had to solve the problem of the Dacians (App. *Bell. Civ.* 3.25, Str. 7.3.5; Aug. *Res Gest.* 30; Dio 49.37). Even if the events are uncertain in detail, the consequences are clear. Mócsy talks both of the 'Celticization' of trans-Danubian populations, especially in Slovakia and the Northern Hungary plain, and of the 'Dacianization' of Northern

Pannonia through intermediaries like the Cotini and Osi who spanned both banks of the Danube bend, and acquired Dacian names while still speaking Celtic (e.g. *CIL* VI 32542, Tac. *Germ.* 43).[6]

In Britain the same phenomena of ambiguity and intermediaries can be compared to the Central European frontiers. Breeze and Dobson's helpful little book on Hadrian's wall stresses the fact that the formal frontier cut through the Brigantes *ethnos* and that the goddess 'Brigantia' had dedications as far north as Birrens in Dumfrieshire.[7] This happened just about at the point when the 'broch' culture was beginning to move southwards and was overlapping with the hill-fort region, often violently, and so creating a kind of squeeze on the 'Völker zwischen'. This is what had happened in Germany and Czechoslovakia, and may have had something to do with the odd decision to move up to the Antonine line so soon after.[8]

Several scholars have seen military parallels between what was happening in Britain and the elaborate *fossatum* frontier system begun in Africa at a date which we can begin to say with fair certainty now, as a result of Trousset's work in Tunisia, was Trajanic or Hadrianic.[9] But apart from the military aspect, there is one dominating social and ethnic fact that has become increasingly clear, which is, that the African frontier did not and was not intended to separate the desert from the sown, sedentary from nomadic, or urban settler from montagnard transhumants. On the contrary, the southern *limes* cut across the routes of tribal groups, like the Musulami and Nobadae, and divided them from various fractions of peoples attached to their federations. These fractions were an essential part of their social systems that certainly continued to exist during the period of Roman rule.[10]

Even on the Eastern frontiers of the Roman Empire where it is, of course, obvious that the existence of the Parthian Kingdom created the need for political and military decisions by the Romans that were unparalleled in the West,[11] we can note some places at least where the proposition applies. There is, for instance, the extraordinary difficulty that we have in a later period, when Persia had taken the place of Parthia, in deciding where the *gentes* of the *regiones Transtigritanae* were located and under whose jurisdiction they fell – whether Persia's or Rome's.[12] Further south, the fluidity of the *limes Palaestinae* at all periods seems, just as in Africa, to have been the result of constant movement of Arabian Saracen *ethnoi* in Transjordania across what we might call the Roman 'line of rail' from Aquabah to Bosra.[13] And the Armenian highlands were notorious for their intermediary role throughout Roman history in the East. The villagers in Philostratus' *Life of Apollonius* who lived – or were imagined to live – on the Syrian borders found themselves at one moment ruled by Romans and at another by 'Babylonians' (Philos. *V. Apol.* 1.37). The implications of this in cultural terms are obvious.

B. Given then the objective fact that these were the conditions that existed as the Romans fixed their frontiers by the second century A.D., is it possible that they actually account for and help to explain the logic of Roman frontiers? Some years ago a view was put forward by John Mann which repudiated the very notion of logic playing a part in frontier formation.[14] 'No such thing as a "natural frontier" exists', he argued, as he attacked those who imagined 'a logical and coherent application of something called "frontier policy" – as if each stage represented a refinement and improvement of a well-thought-out basic disposition'.

If we look away from strategic factors, however, and consider economic, ecological and social conditions there is, I believe, a greater degree of logic than Mann would allow. This is the lesson to be drawn from Owen Lattimore's classic study of the Chinese frontier in the third century B.C. from whose works I have framed my second proposition, namely that *frontiers should not be regarded as linear barriers but as 'zones of differentiation'*.[15] That is to say, frontiers are really regions which are marginal because they are mixed both socially and economically, representing as they do the change over from intensive to extensive production, where the capacity to collect food surpluses is offset by social systems that are incapable of producing those surpluses. They are necessarily zones because no state ever arrives at the optimum balance between its range of conquest (i.e. its military capacity) and the economy of its rule (i.e. where the military expenditure is no longer paid for by tax returns); and because the turn-over from economic viability to economic liability is necessarily gradual, unperceived and unstable.

I have adopted this proposition because it seems to me that such conditions fit the evidence we have of Roman frontiers of the Western Empire and perhaps even of parts of the East. Signs of the La Tène *oppida* culture of proto-civitates in Northern Europe gradually peter out and become more scattered on the edges of the North European uplands, just as Germanic intruders were destroying these Celtic territorial units and making it more difficult for organized communities to emerge.[16] In the clay *terpen* regions of Holland north of the Rhine and on sites such as that of Feddersen Wierde in Lower Saxony, we can prove that settlements were only just beginning to form with grain stores, stock enclosures and imported pottery by the first century A.D.[17] Recent surveys of the Solway region of Hadrian's Wall in Britain illustrate the proposition excellently by some very clear statistics. Here as one moves from south to north of the frontier the density and style of the habitation sites of the Carvetti people is transformed from intensive to extensive production.[18]

The 'zone' character of the frontier is clearly visible in the Roman attempt to extend some sort of control, often far beyond the formal line of the *limes* fortifications, to bind in definable 'Vorlimes' areas as the social and economic regimes of the 'free' territories became more stable. One can point to the extraordinary and still mysterious 'Devil's Dykes' or Langwälle earthworks that run for 700 km from Budapest to Belgrade some 100 or 200 km to the east of the Danube *limes* protecting the great Sarmatian plain. Formerly accepted as purely Later Empire defences, they are now thought probably to originate from the first phase of Roman frontier formation in the first century A.D.[19] Almost exactly parallel are the earthworks of the 'Brazda lui Novac' that run from the Iron Gates along the foot of the Carpathians enclosing the Wallachian plain. Like the Hungarian Langwälle, this boundary too used to be dated exclusively to the Later Empire after Dacia had been abandoned, but experts are now beginning to have their doubts and think it could be part of the pre-Trajanic Danube forward zone.[20] A similar 'Devil's Dyke' extending along the west bank of the Rivers Gran and Eipel in South-Western Slovakia, as yet undated, is generally associated with the Quadi.[21]

These various systems – they cannot be called defensive barriers – look very much like limits to Roman protectorates and have naturally been associated with the increasing number of Roman or Romanized buildings and out-posts which keep turning up deep inside the 'Vorlimes' territories. In Moravia, for instance, sites such as Milanovce near Nitra or Staré Mesto near Uberské Hvaidste on the R. Morva are now thought to antedate the campaigns of Marcus Aurelius.[22] Those who believe that Romans in the Later Empire adopted a purely defensive position cowering behind the line of river, despite the evidence of Ammianus Marcellinus (29.62), should note the Roman out-posts at Hatvan-Gombospuszta 60 km beyond the Danube well into *barbaricum* and the military camp at Felsögöd on the right bank, several kilometres away from the river Danube. All this seems to make more credible the much disputed evidence of the *Historia Augusta*, that Marcus Aurelius was contemplating the annexation of two new provinces beyond the Danube of Marcomannia and Sarmatia. And it explains the reasons why on the Rhine the formal *limes* did, in fact, advance well beyond the river into Baden-Würtemberg and Bavaria.

C. The ambiguity of frontier zones leads on to the economic role of the frontier regions in the Roman political economy and to my third general proposition, that *zones of differentiation are by definition zones of symbiotic exchange* – exchange between systems of intensive and extensive production.

Roman policy was to capitalize upon the conditions of inter-dependency of regions on both sides of the frontiers. The export of food to free Germans or to Africans may have begun as a concomitant of luxury gifts, exchange and subsidies to friendly princes. But it quickly created a demand and became a necessity. The policy may even have been deliberate. In China, in the second century B.C. it was claimed as an explicit policy of the Han Dynasty to 'bait' the nomads with a taste for imperial exports of luxuries and food in order to keep them docile.[24] The Germans, although primarily herding communities, always grew some types of grains.[25] Yet, despite the *inopia frumenti* which Caesar himself found in free Germany (*Bell. Gall.* 6.29), grain production in regions like Bohemia actually declined at first after the arrival of the Romans.[26] This was partly because Germanic intruders had destroyed the agrarian organization of the *oppida*. But the implication is that grain could be obtained elsewhere. The increased agricultural production of Roman frontier regions in the lower Mosel-Main, the Wetterau, Picardy and Artois, and in the region of the Agri Decumati between Sinsheim and Baden-Baden, while principally to feed the Roman army, was almost certainly used for export also.[27] A change-over by the early third century from stock-farming to arable in some farms near the frontiers can be demonstrated near Trier.[28]

The Romans in their turn had enormous requirements for leather products (and to a lesser extent, meat) for their armies which could not be met from within the Empire where grazing was relatively scarce.[29] The imposition of a tribute in leather hides upon the Frisians (Tac. *Ann.* 4.72) is an example of one way that the demand was met. Exchange of Roman goods for German cattle was obviously another, and it had a profound economic impact as far away as Scandinavian Gottland.[30] As employment of meat-eating Germans in the Roman army increased, so too meat requirements must have increased.

Not that we should try to see exactly the same sort of exchange relationships in every frontier region. On the Lower Danube, for instance, in addition to the 'enforced colonization' of rural areas in Lower Moesia from the time of Nero, at least, which appears to have been partly to increase the production of corn (cf. *CIL* XIV 3608),[31] we also have the celebrated record of Hunt's *Pridianum* (*BM Pap.* 2851) which can now be fixed to the date of A.D. 105 before the annexation of Dacia.[32] It shows the extensive Romanization of Wallachia and the way that military corn was requisitioned from this region north of the Danube when new troops were being mustered for Trajan's second Dacian War. It is on a par with Gren's study of the Balkan frontiers which argued convincingly that South Russia, Bessarabia and the Crimea, though not formally inside the frontiers, were major suppliers of food to the Roman armies which were garrisoned for this obvious reason, not for defence, along the line of the Danube.[33]

The stimulation of demand for Roman goods among free populations is amply attested although it was not, of course, confined to staples only. Like the Gauls, most free Germans developed a taste for Roman wine (Caes. *Bell. Gall.* 4.2, *contra* Tac. *Germ.* 23). The export of Roman *terra sigillata* and other pottery or ornaments, as well as more substantial treasures, of bronze, silver and gold into free Germany have been amply documented.[34] Vice versa the Romans almost certainly benefited from the development of high quality iron production among the Germans.[35] The prosperity and scale of Roman imports at an iron-producing site like Feddersen Wierde near Bremerhaven must explain the corresponding decline of iron production south of the *limes* in the Hunsrück territory of the Treveri during the first two centuries of Roman occupation.[36]

The exchanges, as we know, were closely controlled by the Romans. The Hermunduri, in Tacitus' day, were exceptional in being permitted to enter deep into Roman territory (Tac. *Germ.* 41), although the imposition of *commercium in ripa* – fixed days and places for trading – for the first time by Marcus Aurelius upon the

Marcomanni in A.D. 175 suggests that other allies too had previously had this
privilege from time to time.[37] By and large, however, there is no reason to think that
most exports beyond the frontiers took place either through 'barbarian' agencies or
even necessarily through private Roman entrepreneurs, since a good many of the
high value Roman goods which have turned up in German graves (like those of the
Lübsow group in Pomerania, for instance, or the 'Opferfunde' of Jutland) appear
to be the consequences of diplomatic gifts and/or as payments for military
services.[38] And raiding cannot be excluded.

There is, however, one important distinction between the type of luxury good
and the exchange of staples described above, which has been noticed in recent
studies:[39] that is, the apparent separation of the zones in which the two categories of
export operated. Using Egger's distribution maps of western frontiers one can
detect a 'buffer zone' of about 200 km immediately to the north of the frontiers, just
about the same as the zone covered by the *oppida* culture, where there is a relative
absence of finds of luxury articles, in marked contrast to the far north. As far as one
can see on the eastern frontier, where the picture is complicated by the changing
status of Dacia within the Roman Empire, the same contrast existed between the
regions north and south of the Carpathians and Transylvanian plain, if one
examines a distribution map of Roman coins and imports.[40]

This underlines the conclusion that, while economic inter-relations and cultural
assimilation of the border regions north and south of the frontiers were increasing,
at the same time the division of economic activity between the sectors became
progressively more marked.

D. And that brings me to my final proposition, that *frontiers are by their marginal
nature necessarily agents of change.* The very stability and the economic
stimulation of the exchanges alters the marginality of both the economic and
military balance.[41] In the case of the Roman Western front where the evidence is
clearest and best studied the effect upon the 'barbarian' communities to the north in
the buffer zones and beyond was little short of dramatic. The Marcomanni in
Bohemia in the first to second centuries are an example of the political centralism
and population increase made possible by the accumulation of wealth from trade
and gift exchange. Although this has sometimes been doubted as a typical example,
recent studies of settlements and housing of the Dutch *terpen* in regions such as
Drente and Friesland can leave no doubt of the growth of economic and social
differentiation of communities in Holland in the second and third centuries A.D.
At Fedderson Wierde on the Weser, for example, Haarnagel's tables show that the
number of houses in the village of a primarily herding community more than
trebled between the first and third centuries A.D. and that the population within an
area of about 24 km² rose by a similar amount.[42]

The development of 'Herrenhof' houses and the large 'Bauernhof' type in villages
like Fochteloo (Friesland), the latter house often associated with smelting and

forging of iron and containing most of the imported *terra sigillata*, gives us a clue as to how these societies were organised.[43] At Wijster (Drente) the process is the same although starting slightly later. The considerable prosperity of North Holland beyond the frontiers in the second century A.D. is reflected in the fact that there have been more Roman silver coins found there than in the Brabant, which lay within the Roman frontiers.[44] Sometime early in the latter half of the second century A.D. the Carpi or pre-Carpi inhabitants of the Carpathians in 'free' Dacia began to move down from the mountains into the agriculturally rich plain of Moldavia, settling at sites like Poiana-Dulcesti.[45]

Close contact with the Roman frontiers, therefore, altered the character of the populations beyond, particularly those in the buffer zones. Increases in population as well as greater stability of political organization and settlements created greater demands for food. Already in the Early Empire, as the examples in the introduction show, attempts were made to expand onto land in the Roman provinces. Some of them were successful by agreement with the imperial government.

Immediate needs might have been satisfied by border raids. But the frontiers were, of course, designed to prevent exactly this. Employment within the Empire sometimes eased the strain on resources. In Africa, for instance, careful regulations to allow seasonal labourers across the borders before the harvest, but to permit transhumant herds to enter only after the crops had been gathered, probably explain the double frontier system which evolved there and the inscriptions of 'port' tariffs we possess.[46] The best attested form of migrant labour was for employment in the Roman army. To the Germans, as Fustel de Coulanges once observed, the Roman Empire was not an enemy but a career.[47]

So we might sum up by saying that the Roman Empire on the eve of the barbarian invasions of the late second and third centuries A.D. had reached the natural limits of its useful economic expansion. Yet the very process of stabilization had created dependent but expanding politics beyond the frontiers which were bound to destroy the conditions for their own existence. The frontier history of the Later Roman Empire then becomes the history of a struggle for finite resources, a competition for the food produced in the frontier zone, while at the same time there was a less efficient use of the resources available.

So, on the one side there was a rising population of Frisians, Chauci, Chamavi, Hermunduri, now appearing in the third century under new names and in new political clothes as Saxons, Franks, Alamanni, etc. supplemented by the arrival of new populations who were attracted by the very prosperity and the produce of frontier zones. We can see this for instance in the advance of the Tcherneachow-Sîntana de Mureș culture spreading across the Lower Wallachian plain and into Transylvania[48] – almost certainly the Goths; or in the building of the *valla* of Athenaric in Moldavia and Besserabia across the mouth of the Dneister trying to keep off the nomadic Steppe Huns;[49] or in the occupation of the *Agri Decumates* by Burgundians and Alamans. All of these are evidence of assaults upon the regions which supplied the Roman army. In the West the 'Late Roman Transgression' of climate, if a reality, would have put still more pressure on the rising population and food resources by flooding many of the grazing lands of Northern Europe. Meanwhile, the evidence from Wijster and the clay *terpen* of Holland shows that they reached their densest population in the period 360-395.[50]

On the Roman side, too, the number of months to feed increased considerably, principally through changes in the size and organization of the army in the fourth century, at the very time when the means of supplying the army became more difficult. At a conservative estimate, the numbers of military personnel in the frontier regions had doubled since the second century.[51]

Even before the reforms of the Later Empire, the normal four legions of the German frontier (c. 20,000 legionaries), plus auxiliaries, would have required something over 10-12,000 metric tons of grain per year; that is, the tithe of the produce of about 40,000 sq. miles, which could not possibly have been met from the two German provinces alone (about 20,000 sq. miles), even if there had been nothing but *arvi primi* in those provinces. But to make matters worse, there was also a sharp rise in the use of cavalry in the Later Empire, particularly after Adrianople in 378, as Vegetius makes clear (Veg. *Epit. rei milit.* 1.20).[52] Yet a horse requires about four times as much area of land to produce fodder as that needed to produce corn for an infantryman.

The corn route from Britain to the Rhine army must have suffered continual interference. Sea-borne raids of Saxons, Salian Franks and Frisians were impossible to prevent despite the Saxon Shore defences of the late third century and also the campaigns of Julian and Count Theodosius in the fourth century to drive out the Chamavi and other groups of Franks from South Holland. Hence the desperate effort to keep open the line of the Rhine-Waal and the *limes Belgicus*.[53] Similarly, if it is correct that the Balkan armies had regularly imported some grain from South Russia and from the provinces of Asia, it needs no imagination to perceive the effect of Gothic raids over the Eastern Mediterranean in the third century and of the later invasions of the steppe nomads. The destruction of Novae in the third century gives some idea of what happened.

The considerable development of the grain-rich regions of Scythia Minor in the later Empire, and what appears to be an era of local prosperity and production, judging by the size of a town like Slava Rusa, gives some evidence of the efforts made by the state to meet new internal demands.[54] But the new prosperity of these regions inevitably attracted in their turn the attentions of hungry invaders. Almost every invasion in Eastern Europe from the late second to the fifth century was launched through the Dobrudja.[55]

It is this competition for resources, for food most of all, which was the main dynamic of Later Imperial frontier history. There was devastation of land on both sides which intensified the need. In Roman territory terms like *vastatum Illyricum, Moesia deperdita, Galliae turbatae* (Hist. Aug. *Aurel.* 39.7, *Prob.* 13.5-6) are given credibility by the archaeological evidence of 50% of known *vici* and villas in Northern Gaul being abandoned.[56] In retaliation, and sometimes explicitly to recoup agrarian losses of cattle and corn (e.g. Hist. Aug. *Prob.* 13.8 into Germany), the Romans raided deep into *barbaricum*. We know from Ammianus Marcellinus that Valentinian's invasion of Quadi and Sarmatian lands in 374/375 created *ciborum inopia* (Amm. Marc. 30.6.2). Coin hoards of the country to the north of the Middle Danube show a close correlation with invasion dates and retaliatory raids.[57] Ammianus also comments on the special problems of fodder for the nomadic Alans arriving from the Russian steppes (31.2.18ff.). It has been argued by some, plausibly, though not certainly, that the breakdown of Roman cadastration systems in the *Agri Decumates* is an indication of a drop in agricultural production.[58] And Jordanes describes the once productive grain regions in Wallachia, now settled by Goths, as 'rich in nothing except flocks and pastures for cattle ... but not fruitful in wheat or any other sort of grain' (*Get.* 51.267).

The inevitable consequence was famine and shortages. How many soldiers and horses of the frontiers were like those described by Libanius in 380/81 'starving and shivering for lack of food' (*Or.* 2.37)? How typical was the *dux* of Cyrenaica, Cerealis, who sold off all the horses of his unit of mounted archers (Synes. *Ep.* 131)? In both these cases the cause is put down to corrupt officials and traders, but as we know from studies of famine in England, these kinds of middle man are always selected as useful scapegoats to divert the anger of people away from failures of the state.[59]

On the barbarian side the voices of our sources are deafening in their report of shortages. In 269 the Goths invading Macedonia were short of supplies and dying of hunger (Zos. 1.45-6). In 332 the desperation of the Visigoths, who were suffering from acute famine (*Exc. Val.* 6.31), is summed up in the *foedus* agreed with Constantine offering them military service and *annona* (Jord. *Get.* 21.112), probably renewing earlier contracts (Jord. *Get.* 16.89). The same agreement had been made earlier with the Vandals, who, in return for service, were permitted markets on the Danube (Dexippus fr. 7). Famine, as every source notes, was the prime cause of the great Gothic invasions of 376 – 'lacking the necessities of life' (*attenuata necessariorum penuria*, Amm. Marc. 31.3.8). The diversion of food produce from the relatively rich agrarian areas of Pannonia (Jord. *Get.* 29.146; cf. *Exposit.* 57) to feed Rome and Italy, when they were cut off from Africa in the late fourth century, may well explain why Alaric and his federate Goths, who were by then settled inside Pannonia, were forced to move south.[60]

Not surprisingly in view of their own shortages, the Romans grew increasingly reluctant to export food to the free territories. Although literary sources often portray this as purely punitive action for security reasons, the truth is that there was not enough food. The best known example is that of A.D. 175, when Marcus Aurelius restricted all trading activities across the Danube (Dio 71.15-16 and 19). The effect upon the Marcomanni was catastrophic. By 180 'because of the numbers of them that were dying and through the constant ravaging of their territory, they had no food or men any longer' (Dio). Yet the terms inflicted upon them in this abject state was to furnish annual amounts of grain *to the Romans* – a demand they obviously failed to meet (Dio 72.2.1-2). Later, the unstable conditions which gave support to Procopius' rebellion in 365 were probably linked to shortages and famine in the Roman provinces of Asia and Thrace, noted by Themistius (*Or.* 7). At more or less the period of the Marcomannian wars the first legislation appeared forbidding the export of iron, wheat and salt to the 'enemy' (*Dig.* 39.4.11). The same treatment was probably dealt out to the Western Germans of the Ems-Weser-Elbe line, where coins hoards indicate disturbed conditions in the same period and where one can point to the cutting off of the export of *terra sigillata* in the third century. Roman coins cease to be exported to Thuringia in the third century and slightly later to the regions north of the Brabant.[61] Further north in Scandinavia the absence of Roman imported ware from the third century onwards probably corresponded with the termination of leather exchanges. Even the 'inhospitable and savage Scythian (i.e. Hun)', says Themistius in the later fourth century, who 'has chosen a vagrant life' nevertheless had to 'live by importing the fruits of agriculture from others' (*Or.* 30.350a). And if he could not, he moved to where he could.

Attempts by the Romans to construct a symbiotic but discreet relationship on either side of the borders had failed. Yet the frontiers remained zones where the basic resources had to be either exchanged or fought for. Roman emperors inevitably believed it their duty to fight if they could. But by using the weapon of restricted resources they simply increased the desperation of those whom they deprived. The *foedus* of Constantine and his predecessors was foolishly repudiated by Valens in 367 when he cut off the markets from the Goths. 'The emperor', says Themistius with misguided enthusiasm, 'has removed their normal rations (*siteresion*) ... he has checked their licence to have trade and markets (*emporias kai agoras*) which the previous peace permitted whenever they wanted' (*Or.* 10. 135 a-d). The Codes illustrate the increasing use of restricted trade and distribution; e.g. *CJ* IV.41.1 (375/8) – wine, oil and liquamen; *CJ* IV.63.4 and 6 (Honorius and Theodosius) – general contacts with Persians; *CJ* XII.45.1 = *CTh* VII.16.3 (420) – all *merces illicitae*. Valens's punishment of the Goths is said by Ammianus to have been the main reason for their desperation (*ultima necessariorum inopia*, 27.5.7).

The inability of the barbarians to find markets explains their demand for land under almost any conditions, and hence the force of the invasions when they came. The Goths in migration 'were looking for more fertile land' (Jord. *Get.* 4.27). The celebrated example of starving Goths, so desperate for land in Thrace that they sold themselves into agrarian servitude for food – one dog for one slave – was repeated as a cautionary tale (Amm. Marc. 31.4-5, Jord. *Get.* 26.134-5). But they were no isolated example. Sale of someone *in fame oppressum* seems to have become standard in Romano-Germanic law (e.g. Cap. XVII of the *Collectio Iuris Romano-*

Visigothici, MGH, leg. sec. 1.1. p. 471).[62] New villages in the Meuse valley and in Picardy on farming land of former villas are thought to be evidence of laetic and other forms of servile labour drawn from people like Franks and Alamans.[63] Some of them were prisoners taken in wars, but, as the Emperor Julian observed, there was no need for wars against the enemy when there were slave traders to do the job for him (Amm. Marc. 22.7.8). The size of these mass settlements of barbarians on land within the frontiers represents a major demographic movement and cannot be explained away as the consequences of mere marauders. Immigration across the Rhine left whole regions like Westfalia in free Germany underpopulated for two centuries afterwards.[64]

The settlements of federates within the frontiers was the final step taken by the Emperor Theodosius at the end of the fourth century. For the Roman state the earlier establishment of *laeti, dediticii, gentiles* etc. as dependent labour upon the land was a means of maintaining their own productive capabilities.[65] But allocation of whole regions to autonomous and taxfree federates simply diminished the state's surplus resources, thereby transferring them to the barbarians and extending the marginal frontier zone deeper and deeper into the Empire. As more and more mounted troops entered Roman service and territory, drawn from new nomadic populations, such as Alans and Huns, their needs for extensive agriculture of fodder inevitably increased. A force of 10,000 Huns, for example, such as that which the Emperor Honorius proposed to employ in 409, required large land resources and we know something of the supply problem this entailed (Zos. 5.50). A treaty between Theodosius and the Huns on the Danube significantly made specific mention of the grazing cattle and herds (of horses) (Zos. 4.34). Equally inevitably the intensive farming of cereals diminished and with it the state's reserve of power. In the end, Alaric and Athaulf with their Goths and Huns forced their way first into Italy and then into France in search of food. They were prepared to spare the sack of Rome in return for an annual allowance of grain, which the emperor would not or could not concede.

E. To conclude, the view promoted by Alföldi concerning the 'moral barriers' of Roman frontiers certainly did not extend to economic, technological or cultural exchange.[66] We ought not to be misled by the typically classical, perhaps originally Hellenistic ideology expressed by writers like Appian (*proem* 7) and Aelius Aristides (*Roman Orat.* 80-84) of a great wall enclosing the Empire and separating it off from 'barbarians' – not even if emperors themselves sometimes actually believed their own propaganda.[67]

In reality and in practice, as Lattimore's exposé of the Great Wall of China showed, the symbiotic economies of such border regions, and the free passage through the frontiers necessary to maintain such symbiosis, generates a 'frontier pull' which is stronger than any ideology. What Cooter has more recently called 'interaction spheres' and 'institutional corridors of power', caused frontier barriers to crumble.[68] They crumbled not because of dark eruptions of new barbarian hoards, even if that contributed, but because frontiers are always zones, constantly shifting and in ferment, ambivalent in their loyalties and often having more in common with the 'other side', as it were, than with their own political centre. One of the major factors in creating this ferment was food and trade in staples.

Cambridge   C. R. WHITTAKER

NOTES

*See the bibliographic note at the end for many of the references in this paper. I am grateful to Peter Brunt for comments on an earlier version of the paper, as I am to the participants of the Economic Congress at Budapest.

1. E.g. J. C. Mann, 'The frontiers of the principate', *ANRW* II.1 (1974) 508-33 at 531: 'Hadrian's wall had neither strategic nor tactical value'.

2. B. D. Shaw, 'Fear and loathing: the nomad menace and Roman Africa' in C. M. Wells (ed.), *L'Afrique romaine*, Rev. Univ. Ottawa 52.1 (1982) 25-46 at 40 for criticism of E. N. Luttwak, *The grand strategy of the Roman Empire* (1976); the concept is accepted by G. D. B. Jones, 'Concept and development in Roman frontiers', *Bull. J. Rylands Library* 61 (1978) 115-44.

3. H. J. Eggers, E. Will, R. Joffroy, W. Holmquist, *Kelten und Germanen in heidnischer Zeit* (1964); C. M. Wells, *The German policy of Augustus* (1972) ch. 2; J. Filip, *Celtic civilization and its heritage* (2nd edit. 1977), with maps provided.

4. R. Hachmann, G. Kossack, H. Kuhn, *Völker zwischen Germanen und Kelten: Schriftquellen, Bodenfunde und Namengut zur Geschichte des nördlichen Westdeutschlands um Christi Geburt* (1962).

5. F. C. Hawkes, 'The Celts: report on the study of their culture and their Mediterranean relations' in *Le Rayonnement des civilisations grecques et romaines sur les cultures périphériques* (8ᵉ Congrès int. d'arch. class., Paris, 1963) 61-79.

6. A. Mócsy, *Pannonia and Upper Moesia* (trans. S. Frere) (1974) 28, 57.

7. D. J. Breeze and B. Dobson, *Hadrian's Wall* (1976) 43.

8. D. J. Breeze, 'Roman Scotland during the reign of Antoninus Pius' in *XII Congress Frontier Studies* (1980) 46.

9. P. Trousset, *Recherches sur le limes Tripolitanus* (1974) 146ff.; cf. G. D. B. Jones and D. J. Mattingley, *Britannia* 11 (1980) 323-26.

10. Discussed at length by me in C. R. Whittaker, 'Land and labour in North Africa', *Klio* 60 (1978) 331-62 and more recently by Trousset, 'Rome et nomadisme: mythe et réalité' in *XII Congress Frontier*

Studies (1980), and Shaw (n. 2) – the latter points out the military absurdity of a *fossatum* with gaps of up to 70 km wide, if the intention was merely to exclude.

11. J. G. Crow and D. H. French, 'New research on the Euphrates frontier in Turkey' in *XII Congress Frontier Studies* (1980) point out the uniqueness of the *ripa* defences on the Turkish Euphrates, but even here there is doubt as to what forward frontier system Corbulo used in relation to the *ripa* defences.

12. B. H. Warmington, 'Objectives and strategies in the Persian War of Constantius II' in *XI Limeskongress* (1976) 509-20, at 510.

13. E.g. D. F. Graf and M. O'Connor, 'The origin of the term Saracen and the Rawwafa inscriptions', *Byz. Stud.* 4 (1977) 52-66 for clear parallels with Numidian confederations and the 'double frontiers' from the second century A.D.; again note the gaps of up to 60 km in the frontier 'system'. E. W. Gray, 'The Roman Eastern limes from Constantine to Justinian', *PACA* 12 (1973) 24-40 at 28 perceives Roman strategy in relation to Palmyra as being one of cutting across the lines of transhumance.

14. Mann (n. 1).

15. O. Lattimore, *Studies in frontier history* (1962) esp. 113. It was only after the completion of this paper that my attention was drawn by Barri Jones to the remarkable model of frontier economies by Prince Gorchakov to account for Russian frontiers in Central Asia during the nineteenth century. The model which anticipates Lattimore's famous work is now discussed by W. Kirk, 'The making and impact of the British imperial North-West Frontier in India', in B. C. Burnham and H. B. Johnson, *Invasion and Response* (B.A.R. 73, 1979) 39-55, esp. 52-3.

16. Hachmann (n. 4) Karte 2.

17. H. Jankuhn, 'Siedlung, Wirtschaft und Gesellschaftsordnung der germanischen Stämme in der Zeit der röm. Angriffskriege', *ANRW* II.5 (1976) 65-126 at 94-5.

18. See G. D. B. Jones in B. C. Burnham, H. B. Johnson (edd.), *Invasion and Response: the case of Roman Britain* (B.A.R. 73, 1979) 62-6.

19. S. Soproni in *X Limeskongress* (1977) 343-97; but K. Horedt in *IX Congrès sur les Frontières* (1974) 209-11 has excavated a section near Arad on the river Mureş which contain infilling of pottery from the 3rd and 4th century and thus presumably predates later imperial defences. The notion of a 'zone' is obviously intimately linked to the role of native princes in the border lands; their intermediary status both as *membra partisque imperii* (Suet. *Aug.* 48) extending outwards yet as representatives of non-Romans intruding inwards underlines the ambiguity of frontiers. The subject has been recently well studied from this point of view by D. C. Braund, who is shortly to treat it in a book.

20. The discussion of the valla of Wallachia is summarized by Vulpe in *IX Congrès sur les Frontières* (1974); but for doubts over later dates see Horedt (n. 19) 211-14 and I. B. Cataniciu in *XI Limeskongress* (1977) 339-40.

21. I have not been able to read F. Römer, *Les fosses du diable en Hongarie* (1876).

22. Mócsy (n. 6) 89-91 thinks they are villas of Roman client princes, but see T. Kolnik in *XI Limeskongress* (1977) 181-97 for other possibilities in the Later Empire of supply centres and *mansiones*.

124 C. R. WHITTAKER

23. Soproni in *8th Congress Limesforschung* (1974) 197-203. This kind of evidence seems to me to destroy the model of river border defence proposed by Luttwak (n. 2) fig. 3.2.

24. M. G. Raschke, 'New studies in Roman commerce with the East', *ANRW* II.9 (1978) 640-1361 at 765.

25. W. A. Van Es, *Wijster, a native village beyond the imperial frontiers* (1967) 403.

26. K. Motykova, 'Die ältere röm. Kaiserzeit in Böhmen im Lichte der neueren hist.-archäol. Forschung', *ANRW* II.5 (1976) 178.

27. Ch. M. Ternes, 'Die Provincia Germania Superior im Bilde der jüngeren Forschung', *ANRW* II.5 (1976) 958-63.

28. E. M. Wightman, *Roman Trier and the Treviri* (1970) 188.

29. E. Stevens in M. M. Postan (ed.), *Cambridge economic history of Europe*, I (1966) 94.

30. U. E. Habgerg, *The archaeology of Skedemosse* (1967) 121.

31. A. G. Poulter in *XII Congress Frontier Studies* (1980) 729-44.

32. A. Radulescu and M. Barbulescu, 'Sur les legats du Trajan en Mésie inférieure entre 103 et 108 de n.è.', *Dacia* 25 (1981) 353-8 – my thanks to John Wilkes for the reference.

33. E. Gren, *Kleinasien und der Ostbalkan in der wirtschaftlichen Entwicklung der röm. Kaiserzeit* (1941) 139-45.

34. H. J. Egger, *Der röm. Import im freien Germanien* (1951), analysed by L. Hedeager, 'A quantitative analysis of Roman imports in Europe north of the limes' in K. Kristiansen, D. Paludan-Müller (edd.), *New directions in Scandinavian archaeology* (1977).

35. Ternes (n. 27) 963.

36. Jankuhn (n. 17) 117-19, Wightman (n. 28) 163-4.

37. At Cifer-Pac, one of the trans-Danubian 'Roman' buildings in Czechoslovakia mentioned earlier, which lies along the Amber Route north of Carnuntum, the fact that it was found stuffed with Roman goods has led to the suggestion that it was some sort of a supply centre, although in this case dating from the later third or fourth century A.D., Kolnik (n. 22).

38. Cf. M. Wheeler, *Rome beyond the imperial frontiers* (1954) 29, 34, etc.

39. E.g. E. Demougeot, 'La formation de l'Europe et les invasions barbares' I (1969) 278 and Hedeager (n. 34) 206-10.

40. Provided by O. Toropu in *IX Congrès sur les Frontières* (1974) 71-81.

41. See the interesting and important paper by W. Groenman-van Waateringe, 'Urbanization and the north-west frontier of the Roman Empire' in *XII Frontier Congress Studies* (1980), concerning the

stimulation of native urban economies by the needs of the Roman armies of the frontiers. But G-van W wrongly thinks such stimulation was confined to the Roman provinces.

42. W. Haarnagel in E. v. Lehe (ed.), *Geschichte des Landes Wursten* (1973) 79-80.

43. Jankuhn (n. 17) 94-5, 116-19.

44. Van Es (n. 25) 367, 547.

45. Gh. Bichir, *The archaeology and history of the Carpi from the second to the fourth century A.D.* (B.A.R. S 16, 1976).

46. Whittaker (n. 10) 335, 346.

47. M. Waas, *Germanen im röm. Dienst* (1965) *passim.* For the interchange of recruits to and from either side of the frontier see D. L. Kennedy 'Parthian regiments in the Roman army' in *XI Limeskongress* (1976) 521-31.

48. The standard work is I. Ioniță, *Probleme der Sîntana de Mureş-Černjachov Kultur auf dem Gebiet Rumäniens* (*Studia Gotica*, 1975).

49. Vulpe (n. 20); cf. Amm. Marc. 31.3.5-7.

50. Van Es (n. 25) 367.

51. Precise figures are impossible and often exaggerated. See my comments (in relation to taxation) in C. E. King (ed.), *Imperial revenue, expenditure and monetary policy in the fourth century A.D.* (B.A.R. S 76, 1980) 8. The extremes are laid out by R. Macmullen 'How big was the Roman imperial army?' *Klio* 62 (1980) 451-60, but his conclusion that the army of the Later Roman Empire was only 'a little larger' than the Severan army is as speculative as the rest and against the run of the evidence.

52. G. L. Cheeseman, *The auxilia of the Roman imperial army* (1914) 168 estimated c. 80,000 mounted auxiliaries in the second century, but since then more auxiliary units have come to light. The best guess I can make from the late fourth century *Notitia Dignitatum* with all its imperfections is c. 150,000 cavalry, including *comitatenses*. For the swing to cavalry, see M. M. Roxan, 'Pre-Severan auxilia named in the Notitia Dignitatum', in R. Goodburn, P. Bartholomew (edd.), *Aspects of the Notitia Dignitatum* (B.A.R. S 15, 1976) 59-68 at 61.

53. J. Mertens in *XI Limeskongress* (1977) 65-7.

54. Al.-S. Stefan, 'Recherches de photo-interprétation archéologiques sur le limes de la Scythie Mineure à l'époque de Bas-Empire', in *IX Congrès sur les Frontières* (1974) 95-108 at 105; A. V. Radulescu, 'Quelques aspects de l'activité artisanale le long du limes scythique' *X Limeskongress*, 387-92.

55. C. Scorpan, *Limes Scythiae. Topographical and stratigraphical research on the late Roman fortifications on the Lower Danube* (B.A.R. S 86, 1980) 193-201.

56. E. Wightman, 'Peasants and potentates: an investigation of social structures and land tenure in Roman Gaul', *Am. J. Anc. Hist.* 3 (1978) 125 notes the decline in the Hunsrück adjoining the Moselle; R.

C. R. WHITTAKER

Agache, 'La marque de Rome dans le paysage du nord de la France' in R. Chevallier (ed.), *Influence de la Grèce et de Rome sur l'occident moderne* (1977), describes the same for Artois and Picardy.

57. J. Wielowiejski in *X Limeskongress* (1977) 417-27.

58. R. Koebner in M. M. Postan, *Cambridge economic history of Europe*, I (1966) 36.

59. J. Walter, K. Wrightson, 'Dearth and the social order in early modern England', *Past and Present* 71 (1976) 22-41. Roxan (n. 52), notes a possible case of mounted auxiliary troops being turned into infantry.

60. J. M. Wallace-Hadrill, *The barbarian West 400-1000* (rev. edit. 1966) 23.

61. Wheeler, (n. 38) 28, 89; Van Es (n. 25) 546.

62. Verlinden, *L'esclavage dans l'Europe médiévale*, I (1955) 63-4.

63. G. Raepsaet in *X Limeskongress* (1977) 146-57; Agache (n. 56).

64. W. Janssen, 'Some aspects of Frankish-medieval settlements in the Rhineland' in P. H. Sawyer (ed.), *Medieval Settlement* (1976), 47. G. E. M. de Ste Croix, *The Class Struggle in the ancient Greek world* (1981) Appendix III gives a list of ancient references for such movements.

65. See C. R. Whittaker, 'Labour supply in the Later Roman Empire' *Opus* 1 (1982) 171-9 for a recent discussion with earlier references.

66. A. Alföldi, 'The moral barrier on Rhine and Danube', in *I Congress Frontier Studies* (1952) 1-16.

67. A. R. Birley, 'Roman frontiers and Roman frontier policy', *TAASDN* (1974) 13-25 notes an alternative, persistent ideology of imperial expansion.

68. Lattimore (n. 15) 110; W. S. Cooter, 'Pre-industrial frontiers and interaction spheres: prologomenon to a study of Roman frontier regions' in D. H. Miller, J. D. Steffen (edd.), *The frontier: comparative studies* (1977) 81-107.

BIBLIOGRAPHICAL NOTE

Since 1949 there have been twelve Congresses of Roman Frontier Studies, all of which, except the IVth Congress (held in Durham in 1959), have published their proceedings. Since I have quoted extensively from these reports, I set out their full titles for convenience:

The Congress of Roman Frontier Studies (Durham, 1952)

Carnuntina: Ergebnisse der Forschung über die Grenzprovinzen des röm. Reiches ... 1955 (Graz, 1956)

Limes-Studien: Vorträge des 3. Internat. Limes-Kongresses in Rheinfelden, Basel 1957 (Basel, 1959)

Quintus Congressus Internationalis Limitis Romani Studiosorum 1961 (Zagreb, 1963)

Studien zu den Militärgrenzen Roms: Vorträge des 6. Internat. Limeskongresses in Süddeutschland (Köln, 1967)

Roman Frontier Studies 1967: the Proceedings of the 7th Internat. Congress, Tel Aviv 1967 (Tel Aviv, 1971)

Roman Frontier Studies: 8th Internat. Congress of Limesforschung, Cardiff 1969 (Cardiff, 1974)

Actes du IXe Congrès internat. d'études sur les frontières romaines, Mamaia 1972 (Bucharest, 1974)

Studien zu den Militärgrenzen Roms II: Vorträge des 10. Internat. Limeskongresses in der Germania Inferior (Köln, 1977)

Limes. Akten des XI Internat. Limeskongresses, Székesfehérvar 1976 (Budapest, 1977)

Roman Frontier Studies 1979: Papers presented to the 12th Internat. Congress of Roman Frontier Studies (B.A.R. S 71, Oxford, 1980)